Homer

Barry B. Powell

Blackwell
Publishing

350 Main Street, Malden, MA 02148-5020, USA
108 Cowley Road, Oxford OX4 1JF, UK
550 Swanston Street, Carlton, Victoria 3053, Australia

The right of Barry B. Powell to be identified as the Author of this Work has been asserted in accordance with the UK Copyright, Designs, and Patents Act 1988.

First published 2004 by Blackwell Publishing Ltd

Library of Congress Cataloging-in-Publication Data

Powell, Barry B.
Homer / Barry B. Powell.
  p. cm. – (Blackwell introductions to the classical world)
Includes bibliographical references and index.
ISBN 0-631-23385-7 (alk. paper) – ISBN 0-631-23386-5 (pbk.: alk. paper)
1. Homer–Criticism and interpretation. 2. Epic poetry,
Greek–History and criticism. 3. Odysseus (Greek mythology) in
literature. 4. Achilles (Greek mythology) in literature. 5. Trojan
War–Literature and the war. 6. Civilization, Homeric. I. Title. II.
Series.

PA4037.P66 2004
883'.01–dc21   2003001873

A catalogue record for this title is available from the British Library.

Set in 10.5/13pt Galliard
by Graphicraft Ltd, Hong Kong
Printed and bound in the United Kingdom
by MPG Books Ltd, Bodmin, Cornwall

For further information on
Blackwell Publishing, visit our website:
http://www.blackwellpublishing.com

To my beloved brother Brian

Contents

Preface

People who are not in Classics, or who are just entering Classics, often ask, "What do we really know about Homer?" This book is for them. I don't assume that the reader knows Greek, but sometimes I will discuss Greek words and concepts because, of course, Homer's thought is encoded in his words. I do assume that the reader has read the *Iliad* and the *Odyssey* in translation, so that my small book will serve as a first reader's introduction and commentary to the texts of Homer.

All things pertaining to Homer can be argued or are argued by someone somewhere. A recent study proposes that the ruins of Troy lie in the British Isles! In this book I will leave aside the "but so-and-so thinks" because you can find someone who thinks almost anything about Homer. Even many professional classicists do not understand the basis to assumptions often repeated about Homer, the most important author in the classical Greek canon by far, so this book will be for them too. Enormous progress has been made in Homeric studies in the last several generations, and I will attempt to explain just where this progress has brought us. I will focus on superior thinkers about Homer, whom even in the cacophony of views most Homerists take to be reasonable. I will not hesitate to present conclusions that I have myself reached after decades of reflection.

The translations of the *Iliad* and the *Odyssey* used in this book are modernized and modified from the Loeb translations of A. T. Murray. The numbers of lines in the translations and in the original do not always correspond.

My thanks to Jim McKeown, who read the manuscript with attention; and to Tom Kostopoulos, who did the same. Silvia Montiglio helped me too. All errors of interpretation or fact are, of course, my own.

Αὐτῷ μοι τί γένοιτο; θεοὶ τιμῶσιν ἀοιδούς.
Τίς δέ κεν ἄλλου ἀκούσαι; ἅλις πάντεσσιν Ὅμηρος.
οὗτος ἀοιδῶν λῷστος, ὃς ἐξ ἐμεῦ οἴσεται οὐδέν.

What might happen to me? The gods honor the *aoidoi*.
Who would hear any other? Homer is enough for everyone.
He is the greatest of *aoidoi*, who will learn nothing from me.
Theocritus XVI, 19–21

Chronological Chart

4000 BC

Sumerian cuneiform writing is developed, ca. 3400

Egyptian hieroglyphic writing and Pharaonic civilization emerge, ca. 3100

3000 BC

Early Bronze Age

Sumerian cities flourish in Mesopotamia, ca. 2800–2340

Minoan civilization flourishes in Crete, ca. 2500–1450

Akkadian empire in Mesopotamia, ca. 2334–2220

Middle Bronze Age begins with arrival of Indo-European Greeks in Balkan Peninsula, ca. 2000–1600

2000 BC

Late Bronze Age (or Mycenaean Age) begins, ca. 1600

Hittite empire rules in Anatolia, ca. 1600–1200

1500 BC

West Semitic syllabic writing invented, ca. 1500 (?)

Trojan War occurs, ca. 1250 (?)

Destruction of Ugarit, ca. 1200

Dark Age (or Iron Age) begins with destruction of Mycenaean cities in Greece, ca. 1200–1100

1000 BC

Greek colonies are settled in Asia Minor, ca. 1000

900 BC

Neo-Hittite cities flourish in northern Syria, ca. 900–700

800 BC

Greek colonies in southern Italy and Sicily, ca. 800–600

Archaic Period begins with invention of Greek alphabet, ca. 800

The *Iliad* and the *Odyssey*, attributed to Homer, are written down, ca. 800–750

Olympic games begin, 776
Rome, allegedly, is founded, 753
Hesiod's *Theogony* is written down, ca. 750–700

700 BC Homeric *Hymns*, ca. 700–500
Callinus, ca. 650
Cyclic poets, ca. 650–500
Age of Tyrants, ca. 650–500
Pisistratus, 605?–527

600 BC Creation of Hebrew Pentateuch during Babylonian
captivity of the Hebrews, 586–538
Cyrus the Great of Persia, ca. 600–529
Xenophanes, ca. 570–460
Pindar, 518–438
Alleged date of the expulsion of the Etruscan dynasty at
Rome and the foundation of the "Roman Repub-
lic," 510

500 BC Persians invade Greece; battle of Marathon, 490
Persians invade Greece again; destruction of Athens;
Greek victories at Salamis and Plataea, 480–479
Classical Period begins with end of Persian Wars, 480
Aeschylus, 525–456
Sophocles, 496–406
Herodotus, ca. 484–420
Euripides, 480–406
Socrates, 469–399
Peloponnesian War, 431–404
Thucydides, ca. 470–400
Plato, 427–348

400 BC Aristotle, 384–322
Philip II of Macedon, Alexander's father, conquers
Greece, putting an end to local rule, 338–337
Alexander the Great, 336–323, conquers the Persian
empire, founds Alexandria
Hellenistic Period begins with death of Alexander in
323

300 BC Mouseion founded by Ptolemy II, 285–246
Apollonius of Rhodes, third century
Livius Andronicus, third century
Zenodotus of Ephesus, third century

200 BC	Aristophanes of Byzantium, ca. 257–180
	Aristarchus of Samothrace, ca. 217–145
	Roman Period begins when Greece becomes Roman province, 146
100 BC	Didymus, first century
	Roman civil wars, 88–31
	Cicero, 106–43
	Vergil, 70–19
	Augustus defeats Antony and Cleopatra at battle of Actium and annexes Egypt, 30
Year 0	Augustus Caesar reigns, 27 BC–14 AD
100 AD	Josephus, 37–100
200–300 AD	Transfer of Homeric texts from papyrus rolls to the codex
925 AD	Oldest surviving complete manuscript of Homer's *Iliad* (*Venetus A*)

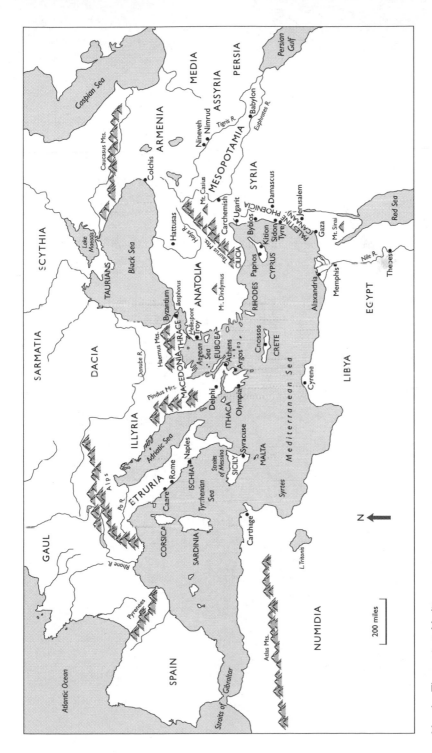

Map 1 The ancient Mediterranean

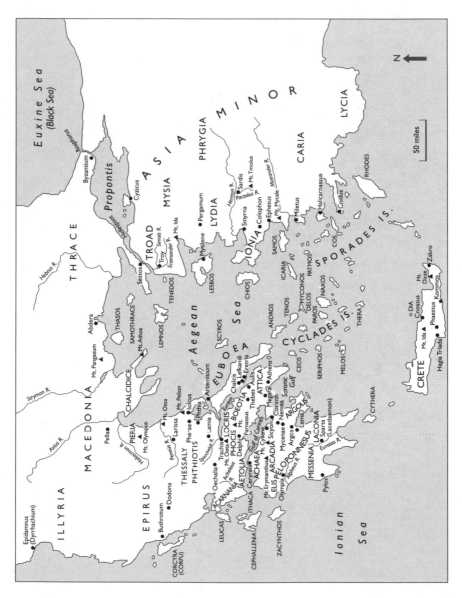

Map 2   Greece, the Aegean Sea, and Western Asia Minor

Introduction

By "Homer" and "Homer's poems" I mean in this book the *Iliad* and the *Odyssey*, attributed to Homer from the earliest times. Was this poet really named Homer? Poems certainly not by the composer of the *Iliad* and the *Odyssey* were attributed to "Homer," but they were later; such false attributions testify to the classic status of the *Iliad* and the *Odyssey*. The name "Homer" must have come from somewhere, most likely because that was the name of a famous poet. The striking systematic silence in the *Odyssey* about events told in the *Iliad*, and such clear efforts in the *Odyssey* to round out the story of the Trojan War as the *Odyssey*'s song about the Trojan Horse (*Od.* 8.499–520), make clear that the singer of the *Odyssey* knew our *Iliad* intimately – in my view because he was the same man.

Not only are the *Iliad* and the *Odyssey* the oldest surviving works of literature in the Western Greek alphabetic tradition, but along with Hesiod's poems they are also the oldest substantial pieces of writing of any kind. Almost nothing survives between these poems – which appear at the dawn of Greek alphabetic literacy – and the rich literary production of fifth-century Athens. Everything else is lost (except for fragments). Why did the *Iliad* and the *Odyssey* not only survive, but also remain the fundamental classics of Western civilization? How and why did they become classics?

We must stand back a moment and ask, what are the *Iliad* and the *Odyssey*? Before anything, they are texts, physical objects capable of corruption, decay, and willful alteration with a history in the material world. They are *things*, which we forget when thinking about their qualities as literature. We want to know how these texts came into being – where, why, and when. This is the *philologist's Homer*, who wants to know what that first text looked like, how it read. Philologists are studying a physical Homer where marks on paper have certain shapes that can be explained in various ways.

Homer is also our richest source of information about early Greece, and because Homer was always a classic, about Greece itself and all that Western culture owes to Greece. There is no such thing as "the Greeks" without the Homeric poems. What does Homer have to say about what happened in the past, about travel, marriage, trade, war, architecture, and religion? Here is the *historian's Homer*, our second Homer, written documents that tell us about the past.

But for most, who are neither philologist nor historian, Homer means the stories that everyone loves and loves to talk about, swept along in the trance of song. It is the stories that make Homer a classic. The *reader's Homer*, our third Homer, is the most important, because he makes worthwhile the labors of philologists and historians.

In part one of this brief book I will examine these three Homers. Working from these perspectives, in part two I will lead the reader through the poems in a kind of gallop, while pointing out on the way the philological, historical, and literary issues that have attracted attention for almost 3,000 years. The further reading section reviews some important secondary literature on Homer.

Part I

Background

1
The Philologist's Homer

Philologists are "lovers of language" and everything about language interests them, but not language as a universally human faculty – linguists do that. Classical philologists are interested specifically in the Greek and Latin languages, or what we can infer about them from the vast number of written pages that survive. The philologist easily forgets that we know nothing directly about the "Greek" or "Latin" languages, however, but are always working with a representation in writing based on them. Writing is a system of conventional symbolic reference, and not a scientific means of representing speech. The distance between writing and speech is therefore very great, as anyone knows who studies French, then travels to Paris.

Greek and Latin speech do not survive, then, but *texts* survive, a Latin word that means "something woven." Many misunderstand Homer in failing to remember that Homer is a text and that texts are in code; speech, by contrast, is not in code (although it may *be* code). Texts are potentially eternal; speech is ephemeral. Texts are material and liable to corruption, distortion, and error; speech is immaterial and disappears immediately. Homer died long ago, but his texts will live forever.

Where did Homer's texts come from? More than anything the philologist would like to answer this question.

What is a Homeric Text?

Texts of the Homeric poems are easy to find, in print constantly since the first printed edition in Florence in 1488. Because it is a material thing, a text has a certain appearance; not only the texture and color of the paper or leather, but also the conventions by which the signs are formed. Early printed editions were set in typefaces made to imitate handwriting in Byzantine manuscripts, an orthographic system (= "way of writing") much changed since ancient times, with many abbreviations and ligatures in which more than one letter is combined into a single sign. Certainly Plato could not have read the first printed text of Homer, nor can a modern scholar without special training, even a professor who has spent an entire lifetime teaching Greek.

In the nineteenth century modern typefaces and orthographic conventions replaced typographic conventions based on manuscripts handwritten in Byzantium before the invention of printing, but in no sense did such modern conventions attempt to recreate the actual appearance, or material nature, of an ancient text of Homer. For example, the forms of the Greek characters in T. W. Allen's standard Oxford Classical Text, first published in 1902, imitate the admirable but entirely modern Greek handwriting of Richard Porson (1759–1808), a Cambridge don important in early modern textual criticism. Complete with lower- and upper-case characters, accents, breathing marks, dieresis, punctuation, word division, and paragraph division, such Greek seems normal to anyone who studies Greek, let us say, at Oxford or the University of Wisconsin today. Here is what the text of the *Iliad* 1.1–7 from the Loeb Classical Library looks like:

μῆνιν ἄειδε θεὰ Πηληϊάδεω Ἀχιλῆος
οὐλομένην, ἣ μυρί' Ἀχαιοῖς ἄλγε' ἔθηκε,
πολλὰς δ' ἰφθίμους ψυχὰς Ἄϊδι προΐαψεν
ἡρώων, αὐτοὺς δὲ ἑλώρια τεῦχε κύνεσσιν
οἰωνοῖσί τε πᾶσι, Διὸς δ' ἐτελείετο βουλή,
ἐξ οὗ δὴ τὰ πρῶτα διαστήτην ἐρίσαντε
Ἀτρεΐδης τε ἄναξ ἀνδρῶν καὶ δῖος Ἀχιλλεύς.

If you study Greek today, and take a course in Homer, you will expect to translate such a version. You are reading "the poems of Homer," you think, but in fact the orthography is a hodgepodge that never existed before the nineteenth century. A full accentual system, only sometimes semantic, does not appear until around AD 1000 in Greek writing and is never used consistently. The distinction between upper case and lower case is medieval. Porson's internal sigma is drawn σ, but in the Classical Period the sigma was a vertical zigzag Σ (hence our "S") and after the Alexandrian Period always a half-moon shape C (the "lunate sigma"); the shape σ appears to be Porson's invention. The dieresis, or two

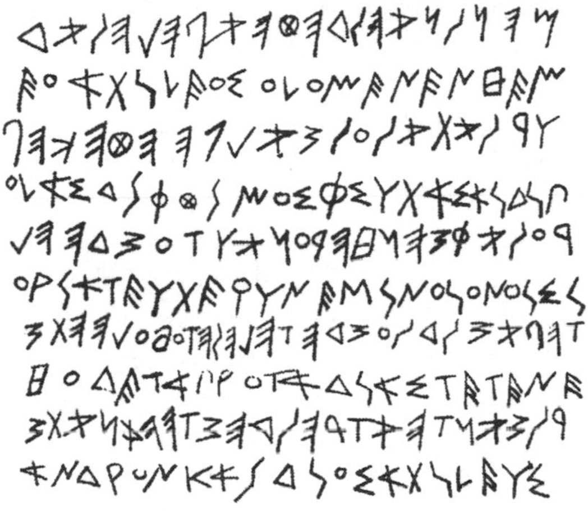

Figure 1   Reconstruction of the first five lines of the *Iliad* in archaic script, written right to left, left to right (after Powell 1991: fig. 7)

horizontal dots to indicate that vowels are pronounced separately (e.g., προϊαψεν), is a convention of recent printing. Periods and commas are modern, as is word division, unknown in classical Greek.

The Oxford Classical Text would have mystified Thucydides or Plato just as much as the first printed text. The much earlier (we might say, original) text of Homer would have puzzled them just as much, which seems to have looked something like figure 1. The direction of reading switches back and forth from right to left, then left to right (called *boustrophêdon* writing, "as the ox turns"). In this earliest form of Greek writing, as we reconstruct it from meager inscriptions, there is no distinction between *omicron* = short ŏ and *omega* = long ō or between *epsilon* = short ě and *éta* = long ē, and doubled consonants are written as single consonants. There are no word divisions, or upper- and lower-case letters, or diacritical marks like accents, or capitals of any kind.

In reading such a text the exchange of meaning from the material object to the human mind takes place in a different way from when we read Homer in Porsonian Greek orthography, or in English translation. The philologist is keenly interested in how this might have worked. Apparently the Greek reader of the eighth century BC was decoding his writing *by the ear*. For this reason the ancient Greek felt no need for word divisions, line divisions, diacritical marks, paragraph markers, or quotation marks because to him (and very occasionally her) the signs represented a continuous stream of sounds. A thousand years after Homer the Greeks still did not divide their words. (In Latin, words were divided from the earliest times, but by no means always.)

When we read Greek (or English), by contrast, we decode the text *by the eye*. We are deeply concerned where one word begins and another ends and whether it is *epsilon* or *êta*. The appearance of our texts is semantic, carries meaning, as when a capital letter says "A sentence begins here" or a period says "A sentence ends here" or a space says "The word ends here." Philologists write articles for or against *êta* = long ē instead of *epsilon* = short ĕ as the correct reading, but for 300 years after the alphabet's invention no consistent distinction was made between the representation of long and short e. Our text of Homer is directly descended from an ancient Greek text, yes, but the text works for us in a different way.

When modern philologists attempt to recover as closely as possible an original text of Homer, as editors claim, they never mean that they are going to reconstruct an original text, one that Homer might have recognized. Rather, they present an interpretation of how an original text might be construed according to modern rules by which ancient texts are explained. What appears to be *orthography* in a modern text of Homer, "the way something is written," is really editorial comment on meaning and syntax. If editors gave us Homer as Homer really was, no one could read it.

The Homeric Question

Still, the philologist's Homer is always the text of Homer, however he might inscribe it. Investigation into the origin of this hypothetical physical object, this text, is the famous "Homeric Question" (from Latin *quaestio*, "investigation"), a central topic in the humanities for over 200 years. When did this text come into being? Where and why? How and by whom? What did it look like? If we only knew where the Homeric poems came from, we would know where we come from, or big parts of us. We are Homer's cultural children.

One way to find the source of something, its origin, is to follow backward, as if going upstream until you find where the water first flows. In physics this source would be the beginning of the universe, but in Homeric studies that spring would be the very first text of Homer. Sometimes people think there must have been "many" first texts, but the variations in surviving versions of our Homer are so tiny that there can never have been more than one first text, the one we are looking for. Let us see what happens when we travel upstream, from now until then.

Our surviving texts are, of course, not very old. The oldest surviving complete text of the *Iliad* is from about AD 925, a beautiful Byzantine manuscript inscribed on vellum. Kept in Venice, it is called the *Venetus A*. Vellum, also called parchment (from the city of Pergamum in Asia Minor where it may have been invented), is a beautiful and sturdy but very expensive basis for a written document. The *Venetus A* was an object of very high material value when it was made.[1]

Like a modern book, the Venetus is made of sewn-bound pages, a form of manuscript we call a codex. Modern books are codices, though the paper has been folded many times into "signatures" before being sewn, then cut at the edges. The codex was invented in the second or third century AD. Earlier texts, including texts of Homer, were not codices, but rolls made of papyrus, in Latin called *volumina*, our "volume." In Greek the word for papyrus is *byblos*, the name of a Near Eastern port from where or from near where came the papyrus that made Homer's poems possible. The 24 "books" of the *Iliad* and the *Odyssey* are really papyrus rolls, the amount that fit conveniently onto a roll. The Homeric poems are texts and their original basis was the papyrus roll.

Side by side with papyrus, the Greeks and Romans wrote notes and composed long works on tablets, usually of wood, hinged at the back with a low depression filled with wax into which the writer would impress the characters. The single mention in all of Homer to writing refers to just such a tablet (*Il.* 6.168, about which more later). Probably most written composition, as we think of it, was done on such ephemeral tablets, although the immensely long Homeric texts must have begun their life directly on papyrus. Most Greek literature survives because at some point what was written on a tablet was transferred to papyrus, an astonishingly durable and transportable substance.

The codex enabled the reader to look things up by paging through the text, as we do today, whereas it was difficult to look something up in a roll. The format of the codex was a kind of barrier between ancient and modern literatures. Unless a work was transferred from papyrus roll to codex in the early Christian centuries, and so leaped the barrier of a changed format, it was lost, as for example was the entire corpus of the obscure Greek lyric poets, little read in the early Christian centuries, including Sappho and Alcaeus (mostly only tiny specks survive on actual papyrus found in Egypt). Perhaps today we experience a similar disjunction between the preservation of information on hard copy and in electronic files, when much is being transferred but much is not. By the time Homer was transferred from roll to codex in the second or third century AD a standard text had been established that we call the "vulgate" or "common" text. Deviations between different manuscripts are small, and there is a fixed number of lines, as far as we can tell. The vulgate of the first few centuries AD is virtually our modern text, if you allow for modern developments in orthography.

Vellum's greater strength (along with its inordinate cost) allowed for a larger page than was possible for a papyrus roll, and the generous margins of the extraordinary *Venetus A* are covered with commentary written in a medieval script called minuscule, the ancestor of our "small letters," as opposed to the "capital letters" in which all Greek manuscripts, including Homer, were until then written. The small medieval script and the large margins allowed scribes to record in the *Venetus A* excerpts taken from scholars who worked in the library of Alexandria in Egypt, founded by the energetic Ptolemy II (285–246 BC), son of Alexander's general, as part of his "temple to the muses," the *Mouseion*. Called *scholia*, these notes offer views on every conceivable topic pertaining to the Homeric poems. Study of the scholia is our only means for reconstructing what Alexandrian scholars of the second and third centuries BC thought about Homeric problems.

Somehow Alexandrian scholars stabilized and regularized the text of Homer, in fact created the vulgate later transferred from papyrus to codex. The original works of Alexandrian scholars are lost, but we may infer their views from the scholia, although the layers of recomposition in the scholia make it impossible to be certain which scholar thought what. Of course, the Alexandrians lived hundreds of years after Homer and had no direct knowledge about him or the origins of his text. The earliest commentator was Zenodotus of Ephesus (third century BC), followed by Aristophanes of Byzantium (ca. 257–180 BC) and his student Aristarchus of Samothrace (ca. 217–145 BC), and in the first century BC the formidable "bronze-gutted" Didymus, said to have written 3,500 books. Philologists would like to work their way back all the way to the text that Homer himself in some way created, but we must admit that we have almost no evidence whatever for the condition of the text earlier than the Alexandrian editors.

Our best evidence for the problems the Alexandrians faced comes from the many fragments of Homer's poems that survive on papyrus found in Egypt (mostly on mummy wrappings for sacred crocodiles), more fragments than from any other author, and two or three times as many fragments from the *Iliad* as from the *Odyssey*. In these fragments there sometimes appear "wild lines" not found in the vulgate that almost always repeat a line or lines found elsewhere or are slight variations of lines found elsewhere. The wild lines seem to have been scribal errors rather than attempts to flesh out, add to, or change the meaning of the text. The wild lines do not represent multiple original versions, then, but are textual corruptions that depend on scribal behavior. Mainly the Alexandrians seem to have removed the wild lines. Wishing to "purify" the text from "false" accretions, they invented several signs still used today, including the *obelus*, a sort of cross in the margin (†) to designate a line suspicious for some reason. There are therefore no collateral lines of descent for the text of Homer, as there are, for example, of the medieval *Chanson de Roland* ("Song of Roland"), which existed in more than one original version. By the first century AD the wild lines have disappeared from the papyrus fragments, as if the authority of an edition produced by the Mouseion had replaced earlier haphazard versions. Perhaps the book trade depended on royal labor or favor; the Mouseion produced the official version and its authority quickly prevailed. Most scholars think that the Alexandrians created the division of the poems into 24 rolls each, although occasional arguments are made for an earlier division.

We have abundant papyrus fragments from Egypt, the earliest being of the third century BC, but before this time there is little direct evidence about what the text might have been like. Quotations by such writers as Plato often differ from the vulgate, but Plato is quoting from memory in a roughshod manner. What is the earliest evidence that the texts of Homer even existed? Herodotus first mentions "rhapsodes" in connection with Sicyon of about 570 BC. Homer must be earlier than that, because rhapsodic performance was not composition but based on memorization of a written, fixed text. The iconoclastic, monotheistic Xenophanes (ca. 560–478 BC) of Colophon, a Greek colony on the coast of Asia Minor, deplores Homer's immoral polytheism: "Homer and Hesiod have ascribed to the gods all that is reproach and blame in the world of men, stealing, and adultery, and deception" (frag. 10 Diehls-Kranz), proving Homer's prominence in Greek education as early as the sixth century BC as an influence to be resisted. The *Homeric Hymn to Apollo*, probably in its present form from a performance on Chios in 522 BC under the sponsorship of Polycrates of Samos, claims to be by "the blind man of Chios," taken to refer to Homer (the myth of Homer's blindness comes from the blind poet Demodocus in the *Odyssey*). The Hymn is not by Homer, but its boastful claim proves again Homer's classic status in the sixth century BC. Certainly full texts of the *Iliad* and the *Odyssey* existed then, according to reports that Hipparchus, the son of Pisistratus (605?–527 BC), tyrant of Athens, instituted a definite order in the presentation of the episodes in the poems at the reformed Athenian patriotic festival of the Panathenaea (more on this topic later). The archaic poet Callinus from Asia Minor seems to be our earliest certain outside reference to Homer, in the first half of the seventh century BC. Callinus refers to the *Thebais*, about the war against Thebes, as a poem by Homer (the poem, of uncertain authorship, is lost). By now we are only 150 years from the date of the invention of the Greek alphabet, which made Homer possible, around 800 BC.

Bellerophon's Tablet: The Arguments of F. A. Wolf

Because the philologist's Homer is the text of Homer, and because the text consists of symbolic markings on a material substance, the Homeric Question is tied to the history of writing. Already in the first century AD Joseph ben Matthias, or Josephus, Jewish general and author of *History of the Jewish War* (AD 75–9), noticed the relevance of writing to the Homeric Question. In an essay *Against Apion* he attacked a Greek named Apion who had challenged the antiquity of the Jews. But the Greeks themselves, complains Josephus, are only a recent people, who had not even learned writing until very late:

> They say that even Homer did not leave behind his poems in writing, but that they were transmitted by memorization and put together out of the songs, and that therefore they contain many inconsistencies. (Josephus, *Against Apion*, 1.2.12)

Because the Greeks were late-comers to writing, Josephus goes on, Homer's very long songs could not have come into existence as we have them. They must be made up of shorter, memorized poems, later written down, and then assembled into the *Iliad* and the *Odyssey*.

Josephus gave no evidence for his views and had none. Only modern scholarship has made possible an accurate dating of the invention of the Greek alphabet and thus an accurate "time after which" (*terminus post quem*) the texts of the Homeric poems could have come into being. European scholars of the eighteenth century had no good evidence to date the origin of the Greek alphabet, but a German scholar (writing in Latin) named Friedrich A. Wolf (1759–1824) argued the same position as Josephus with a vigor and brilliance that has influenced all subsequent Homeric scholarship. Basing his model of analysis on contemporary theories about the origin of the Hebrew Bible through editorial redaction of preexisting manuscripts, Wolf published in 1795 a complex theory about the origin of the Homeric poems in a book called *Prolegomena ad Homerum I.* The *Prolegomena* was intended to precede a critical edition of the text of Homer, but the edition never appeared. Wolf addressed his explanation to the conundrum that whereas Homer exists in writing, descriptions of writing do not seem to appear in his poems:

> The word *book* is nowhere, *writing* is nowhere, *reading* is nowhere, *letters* are nowhere; nothing in so many thousands of verses is arranged for reading, everything for hearing; there are no pacts or treaties except face to face; there is no source of report for old times except memory and rumor and monuments without writing; from that comes the diligent and, in the *Iliad*, strenuously repeated invocations of the Muses, the goddesses of memory; there is no inscription on the pillars and tombs that are sometimes mentioned; there is no other inscription of any kind; there is no coin or fabricated money; there is no use of writing in domestic matters or trade; there are no maps; finally there are no letter carriers and no letters.[2]

We can discount the single apparent exception in Book 6 of the *Iliad*, Wolf argued, where King Proetus of Corinth sends his guest Bellerophon, falsely accused by the queen, to the king's uncle across the sea in Lycia. He gives Bellerophon a folded tablet with "baneful signs" (*sêmata lugra*) (*Il.* 6.178) – presumably the message "Kill the bearer!" As the story continues, King Proetus' uncle could not himself kill his guest–friend Bellerophon because that would be a terrible crime against *xenia*, the customs regulating host and guest. Instead, he sends him to fight the dread Chimera.

"Bellerophon's tablet" carries weight in every discussion of the problem of Homer and writing up to this day. Wolf denies that Homer referred to writing in this passage, because in ordinary usage *sêmata* ("signs"), the word that Homer uses for the marks on the folded tablet, in later Greek never designates characters in writing, which are called *grammata* ("scratchings"). Furthermore, Wolf insisted, in good Greek one never "shows" (*deixai*) writing to someone, as Homer reports. Homer's *sêmata* were therefore symbols not attached to human speech. They are like the *sêmata* in another Homeric passage, where the Achaean heroes make *sêmata* on lots and shake them in a helmet to decide who will fight Hector (*Il.* 7.175ff.). When a lot flies out, the herald does not know what the *sêma* means but must walk down the line until its maker recognizes the *sêma*. Unspoken is Wolf's assumption that "writing" requires a direct relation between graphic symbols and human speech.

We now think of "writing" as being a broader category, being of two kinds, one referring to elements of human speech, or *lexigraphy*, and one communicating in other ways, or *semasiography*. The writing in this book is mostly lexigraphy. The signs *1, 2, 3* are semasiography because they have meaning but do not designate necessary elements in human speech; they are pronounced differently in every language. The Greek alphabet is lexigraphy and icons on a computer screen are semasiography. Homer's *sêmata lugra* in this important passage are undoubtedly semasiographic signs, then, because they bear meaning, but they are not lexigraphic, hence not evidence for the technology that made Homer's poems possible. Wolf did not in any event need to make an exception for the *sêmata lugra*, because his argument depended not on a single ambiguous example, but on the remarkable consistency of Homer's ignorance of writing. Of those who rejected his explanation of *sêmata lugra*, Wolf noted that the phrase "was made more problematic by those who used not to learn Homeric customs from Homer but to import them into him, and to twist doubtful words to fit the customs of their own time."[3]

In the story of Bellerophon's tablet Homer has evidently received from an Eastern source, along with an Eastern story, the folktale motif of the "fatal letter." The motif turns up in the biblical story of David and Uriah the Hittite, whom David sends to the front line with a letter instructing that he be exposed to mortal danger (David wanted to marry Uriah's wife Bathsheba: see 2 Samuel 11.15). Bellerophon's name appears to be formed from that of the Near Eastern storm god Baal. The Lycian king sends Bellerophon against the Chimera, a variation of a dragon-killer myth found already on clay tablets ca. 1400 BC from the international emporium of Ugarit on the Syrian coast near Cyprus: Lycia lies on the coasting route west from Ugarit. So the motif came with the story. Homer knew nothing about "writing": *quod erat demonstrandum*. In Homer's day lexigraphic writing is over 2,000 years old in the Near

East, and we wonder how Homer has remained so ignorant of it that he refers to it a single time in 28,000 lines and then in a garbled fashion. The absence of writing in Homer's world is clear testimony to Hellenic provincialism after the collapse of the Mycenaean world ca. 1150 BC and proof of Hellenic remoteness from the centers of ancient civilization.

The modern shape of the Homeric Question begins with F. A. Wolf because he saw the problem clearly: if Homer knows nothing about writing, how have his poems been preserved in writing? Assuming, as did many (with little reason), that Homer lived around 950 BC, when there was no writing in Greece (another guess), Wolf argued that Homer's poems must have been preserved as songs short enough to be memorized without the aid of writing. In this "oral form," Wolf thought, they were passed down until, when writing appeared later, they were written down. In the sixth century BC in the time of the Athenian tyrant Pisistratus, skillful editors put together the shorter written texts and fashioned our own elegant (but obviously imperfect) *Iliad* and *Odyssey*, Wolf thought.

Wolf's model was parallel to, and inspired by, the discovery in the late eighteenth century that the biblical Pentateuch (= "five-rolls"), the first five books of the Bible, was composed of three or four textual strands skillfully but not seamlessly melded at the hands of editors, no doubt during the captivity of the Jewish elders in Babylon (586–538 BC). Although attributed to Moses, the Pentateuch is much too late to be attributed to him meaningfully. Sometime in the sixth century BC Jewish scholars sat at a table with different scrolls before them. Taking now this, now that, these editors combined preexisting inconsistent texts to create the version we have today. Some called God Yahweh (a volcano spirit), others called him Elohim (Semitic for "gods"). That is why he has both names in Genesis, a thesis about the origins of the Pentateuch on which all modern scholars agree.

Wolf's evidence for his theory was complex. Certain superficial dialectal features appear to reflect an Athenian handling or dusting-up of the text. According to Cicero, who lived in the first century BC about 100 years before Josephus, Pisistratus (605?–527 BC) "first put together the books of Homer in the order in which we have them, which before were mixed up" (*de Oratore* 3.137). Cicero seems to mean that the "books," that is the rolls of papyrus, had earlier circulated independently and so could be recited in differing orders, until the time of Pisistratus. Cicero lived 500 years after Pisistratus, but depended on a Hellenistic commentator, who may have known something.

Cicero's remarks seem to accord with the claim from the fourth century BC in the Platonic dialogue *Hipparchus* (probably not by Plato), to which we referred above. There Socrates refers to Pisistratus' son Hipparchus as "the eldest and wisest of Pisistratus' sons who, among the many excellent proofs of wisdom that he showed, first brought the poems of Homer into this country of ours and compelled men called *rhapsodes* at the Panathenaea [the principal Athenian festival] to recite them in relay, one man following on another as they still do now" (pseudo-Plato, *Hipparchus* 228 B). If there was need for a rule to govern how the poems should be read, there must have been times when they were read otherwise, that is, not in order. To Wolf that fact meant that the poems did not up to this time have a unity at all, but existed first in the short pieces suitable for memorization that Homer's life in an illiterate age required.

Whereas most of the poems that went to make up the fresh compilation of the sixth century BC, now called the "Pisistratean recension," were composed by Homer, Wolf thought, some were composed by the *Homeridae*, "descendants of Homer," said in various sources to have lived on the island of Chios. Pindar of the early fifth century BC mentions them. Nothing real is known of the Homeridae, however, except that they recited the poems of Homer and told stories about his life. Their presence on Chios is likely to be the origin of the story that Homer himself, about whom nothing whatever is known, came from Chios. Perhaps Pisistratus got the short poems from the Homeridae that were assembled into our poems, Wolf theorized.

In sum: you cannot have such long poems as the *Iliad* and the *Odyssey* without writing, in spite of exaggerated claims about the mnemonic skills of ancient peoples. Because Homer's world is a world without writing, the poems, which exist in writing, cannot come directly from this world. They must in some way be the product of evolution. They no more owe their present form and meaning to someone named Homer than Moses wrote the early books of the Bible (which describe the death and burial of Moses). The false attributions are parallel. Scholars may disagree about where Homer stands on the evolutionary arc that begins in an illiterate world and ends with the poems we possess, but for Wolf, Homer stood at the beginning of the arc as the creator of the short poems from which Athenian editors made the Pisistratean recension in the sixth century BC, the basis for the text that became the modern vulgate.

No important scholar disagreed with Wolf's model and for over 100 years, throughout the nineteenth century and into the twentieth century, intelligent and devoted men dissected the Homeric poems from every angle to identify the separate songs, or accretions, of which Wolf had proved it to be composed. Even today there are scholars who closely follow Wolf's argument. For example, an editor of the recent three-volume Oxford commentary on the *Odyssey* writes the following about Book 21:

> Schadewaldt is inclined to accept a broad unity of authorship in [Book] xxi, attributing the whole book to A [one hypothetical author] with the exception of eight lines: namely, Telemachus' boast in 372–5 (already rejected by Bérard), whose removal requires the further deletion of the suitor's simile in 376–7 and the first foot and a half of 378 (which will therefore have to be rewritten); and Zeus's thunderbolt in 412–15. The latter is a melodramatic interpolation, as von der Mühll observed.[4]

Wolf's explanation, just like these remarks, is learned, logical, and clever, but, just like these remarks, it is completely wrong. He had put his finger on the essential problem — a written poem from an illiterate age – but few today believe that the Homeric poems came into being as editorial redactions of preexisting texts, as certainly did the biblical Pentateuch. The followers of Wolf, called Analysts because they attempted to break up Homer's texts into their constituent parts, produced interesting theories and complex proofs, but because their premises were wrong their work to a large degree was a waste of time. In a way, the Homeric texts are made up of shorter songs, but they are not redacted texts. They are the creation, from traditional material, of a single human intelligence, Homer's, as the Californian Milman Parry proved in the early twentieth century.

The Oral-Formulaic Theory: The Arguments of Milman Parry

Milman Parry (1902–35) lived a romantic life and died prematurely at age 34 (perhaps a suicide). Parry showed through stylistic studies of the Homeric texts that Homer's literary style was unique and unknown in such poets as the third-century BC Alexandrian Greek Apollonius of Rhodes, author of the *Argonautica*, the first-century BC Roman Vergil, author of the *Aeneid*, or the English John Milton of the seventeenth-century AD. Parry proved that, from a stylistic point of view, Homer composed by means of units larger than the "word," contrary to what we might expect, and that in our terms these units include phrases, whole lines, and groups of lines. Parry thrust a sword between the old view that great poetry is made with slow beautiful words aptly chosen to fit the moment and a modern view that great poetry can be made in other ways. His theories have been more influential than those of any other literary critic of the twentieth century, not just on how we understand Homer, but also how we understand literature itself, its origins and nature.

Parry began with the ancient mystery of the fixed epithet in Homer, so striking and so odd – those unvarying phrases tacked on to certain names that every reader notices immediately. Why is Achilles "swift-footed" even when he is seated, Hector "shining-helmed," Hera "cow-eyed," and the sea "as dark as wine" (unless the Greek epithet *oinopa* means "wine-faced," as some believe)? Many had looked, but Parry was first to notice that such fixed epithets changed not according to narrative context, but according to the place of the name within the rhythm of the line. In other words, the epithet satisfied the needs of the meter, not the needs of the narrative.

By modern analysis, the complicated meter (dactylic hexameter) consists of lines made up of six units (feet), each of which can be a long and two shorts (— ∪∪ = dactyl) or two longs (— — = spondee), except for the sixth and last foot, which only has two beats. The last syllable can be long or short, but was probably felt as a long because of the line ending; that is, the hexameter always ends with a spondee (— —). Homer would have known nothing about any of this, but had a feeling for a unit made up of six principal beats, each followed by two shorter beats or one longer beat, but the sixth principal beat always followed by a single beat. The concept "line" depends on alphabetic writing, which this rhythmical system precedes, yet the rule about the spondee in the sixth foot means there must have been a pause there, or could be a pause there. Homer's audience, too, would have a feeling for this meter and would expect it and enjoy it.

The system of epithets helps make up the metrical line by providing precast units larger than the name or word. The system within the metrical line is elaborate but thrifty: elaborate because of the different epithets assigned to different places in the line, and thrifty because ordinarily only a single epithet exists for any given place in the line. Such rules could have evolved only within an oral environment, where the poet is singing and the audience is listening.

For example, when the poet wishes to fill the last two feet of the line with the name of Odysseus, the hero is called "noble Odysseus" (*dios Odusseus* = — ∪∪ / — —). When he wishes to fill the last two and one half feet of the line, his name is "wily Odysseus" (*polumêtis Odusseus* = ∪∪ / — ∪∪ / — —, commonly with the verb "said" – *prosephê* – more than 70 times). But if in the same position the preceding word ends with a short vowel that needs to be lengthened, then he becomes "city-sacking Odysseus" because "city-sacking" begins with two consonants in Greek and two consonants lengthen the preceding short vowel (*ptoliporthos Odusseus* = ∪∪ / — ∪∪ / — —). Furthermore, in over 90 percent of Homeric verses a curious word break that scholars call a *caesura* ("cutting") occurs in the third foot; that is, the word does not end before or after the foot, but in the middle of it. In fact the third-foot caesura marks a point where set phrases (formulas) tend to meet, one phrase occupying the line before the caesura, and a second phrase occupying the line after the caesura. In order to fill the line after this caesura with the name of Odysseus (a recurring need) the poet uses the set phrase "much-enduring noble Odysseus" (*polutlas dios Odusseus* = ∪ / — — / — ∪∪ / — —).

Because epithets shift not according to narrative context, but according to metrical demands, we must adjust our sense of the semantic value of the epithet, what it "means." The varying repeated epithets of Odysseus may tell us something about his essential character and tie him to a larger body of tales about clever deeds and city-sacking, but they do not drive the narrative forward. As far as the action of the narrative is concerned, they all just mean "Odysseus." Hence Parry's proof had direct bearing on our understanding of what is "poetic" in Homer's poetry. We must also accept that the complex system of formulaic expressions represented in noun–epithet combinations cannot be the work of a single poet, but must have come into being over time through evolution. Homer's poetic language must be "traditional," a word of central importance in this discussion.

By contrast, the poetic language of, say, William Butler Yeats is not "traditional" because Yeats uses words to express his intention, not to fill out the line. Of course, one might say that all language is traditional, otherwise it would be gibberish, but the Homeric language is a special kind of traditional language because it exists within the expectation of six principal longs followed by two shorts or one long and the sixth principal beat always followed by a single beat. There can be no doubt that Homer and Yeats approached the use of adjectives in a different way. Yeats was a "literate" poet and Homer was an "oral" poet. For Yeats, epithets are nontraditional, but for Homer they are part of the machinery by which he generates his narrative. They enable the poet to finish his line in oral delivery and get on with his story, and they are not a necessary part of the story itself. The "theory of oral composition" or the "oral-formulaic theory" is based on evidence from Parry's study of the fixed epithet, but the systematic application of his method to the Homeric text led to enormous perplexities and logical conundrums that still frustrate Homeric studies.

Parry described the noun-plus-epithet combination as a *formula*, a fixed expression with a certain meaning and metrical value and a certain place in the line. Unconscious that he was adopting a convention of alphabetic literacy in his description, which according to Parry's own theory was not the means by which Homer had composed, Parry saw the formula as a fixed "phrase" made up of more than one "word" that worked in the rhetoric of poetry as the "word" does in the rhetoric of prose. In prose a word is a unit of meaning, whereas in Homer's oral poetry a formula is a unit of meaning. We must remember that the theory that speech consists of "words" is a convention of alphabetic literacy, the result of analysis and the making of lexicons.

The proof of Homer's "orality" is the existence of the formula, a device of no value to the literate poet. We can identify formulas beyond noun–epithet combinations, for example such expressions as "then he answered him" attached indifferently to "much-enduring goodly Odysseus," to "Agamemnon king of men," or to "swift-footed divine Achilles" to fill out a line. Many whole lines are formulaic, too, for example "When early rosy-fingered dawn appeared . . ." One in eight lines in the Homeric corpus is repeated somewhere else. All of Homer is formulaic in this way, Parry thought, made up of preset expressions and fixed phrases, although we do not always have enough of the tradition to see the formulas clearly. Only a very long tradition could explain the formulaic basis of Homeric style. Parry was certain that Homer had composed without the aid of writing by means of such a traditional formulaic rhythmical speech. On this point Wolf and Parry agreed: each thought that Homer had composed without the aid of writing.

Eager to go beyond stylistic analysis and find in the contemporary world a model for what Homer may have been like in the ancient world, Parry traveled with his assistant Albert B. Lord to the southern Balkans between 1929–33, storied journeys in the history of literary criticism. There Parry and Lord amassed an enormous collection of recordings of songs by *guslari*, illiterate peasants who sang long songs, including songs about heroic battle and the abduction of women. One type of song told of a man who returned home after many years just as his wife was about to marry another man.

Parry's best *guslar*, Avdo Mejedovich, at Parry's encouragement, sang for recording by dictation a song as long as the *Odyssey* (called *The Wedding of Smailagich Meho*), although he could neither read nor write. Parry's South Slavic field collection, on aluminum discs and aluminum wire, only partly published and today stored in the Widener Library at Harvard, remains the largest field collection ever made of what we now call "oral song." When analyzed, the written versions of the South Slavic songs prove to fall mostly into a ten-beat line, although the South Slavic line does not approach the Greek line for complexity, and there is little evidence for the elaboration and thrift in the use of epithets that Parry found in Homer. Parry's studies, published as short papers in professional journals, made almost no impression until the 1960s, when Albert B. Lord published *The Singer of Tales*, a synthesis of Parry's theories and penetrating work of his own. Long after Parry's death, Lord returned to the southern Balkans in the 1950s to make fresh recordings and sometimes took down the same song from the same singers as he and Parry had recorded 30 years before.

Lord took a keen interest in the lives and social environment of the *guslari*, inseparable from the tradition in which the singing took place. When a boy wished to become a singer, he would apprentice himself to a master singer. Listening to him and practicing alone, the student gradually learned, by unconscious means, the special metrical language of the *guslar*. If he was persistent and had talent, he could himself become a *guslar*, maybe even a great one.

A *guslar* would know several or many songs, but in the *guslar*'s mind the song did not consist of a fixed sequence of words, about which he could know nothing. The "word" is a convention of literacy (just as much as the "line"), an abstraction that linguists cannot define beyond "things listed in dictionaries." (Is it "some times" or "sometimes"?) Master *guslari* claimed to be able to repeat a song exactly, which they heard a single time, "word for word." When challenged, such singers would never sing the same song verbatim, but would keep close to the same sequence of themes. First this happened, then that happened, then that happened, although even so they would embellish and add new material. The sequence of themes was the song, "word for word." Nor does the *guslar* have a concept of the line as a discrete unit with ten beats, although we can analyze written versions in this way.

There is no such thing as verbatim repetition because there is no fixed text, as Lord put it, meaning really that there is no text at all. A text is a physical thing with symbolic markings on it liable to distortion and

corruption and unfaithful copying, what the philologist studies, and
texts have not yet come into being. The *guslar* remade his song each
time he sang, using the resources of his technique of rhythmical singing.
By analogy, Homer must have done something similar, Parry thought.
Homer was an oral poet, a *guslar*.

By drawing an analogy between modern South Slavic *guslari* and
ancient *aoidoi*, "singers," (singular = *aoidos*) as Homer calls them, Parry
and Lord confounded Wolf's conviction that without writing you cannot generate very long poems, while agreeing with Wolf that Homer
had not used writing in the creation of his poems. In any event, Wolf's
attention was not so much on the impossibility of creating long poems
in an illiterate environment as on the impossibility of transmitting them.
The famous instances of "Homer nodding," inconsistencies that had
formed the basis for theories by the Analysts who followed Wolf (because
they sought to reduce the poems to their constituent parts), appear in
Parry's theory as a common feature of "oral style." Neither the *guslar/
aoidos* nor his audience is annoyed when someone makes a mistake
because they are swept along in the thrill of divine song and have no
means of checking it anyway, in an oral environment, or any interest in
doing so. No wonder Homer's style is unique. He was an oral singer
and the *Iliad* and the *Odyssey* are oral song, Parry argued.

Parry's stylistic studies were impeccable and the Parry/Lord analogy
between oral composition in the modern Balkans and in the ancient
world has been a compelling anthropology. Wolf's premises were proven
wrong and his followers therefore misguided. The Homeric poems were
dictated oral texts and they were not redacted from preexisting shorter
texts of various authorship. But if all Homer is formulaic, the proof of
Homer's "orality," where is the brilliance and poetic genius of the
divine Homer? The followers of Wolf had removed Homer from the
equation: no more did Homer "write" the *Iliad* than Moses "wrote"
Genesis. Parry restored Homer and disproved the redacted text, but in
so doing seemed just as much to take away Homer's opportunity for
creativity and greatness. If all his language is traditional, consisting of
formulas and formulaic expressions, then was not Homer more spokes-
man for a tradition than a creator in his own right?

Because the proof that Homer was an oral poet was based on the
existence of the formula, scholars expended great labor to define a
formula, only to discover that "fixed phrases" open into looser phrases,
now called "formulaic phrases," and that formulaic phrases can drift into
almost anything. One scholar showed how one formula, *pioni dêmôi*,

"[hidden] in rich fat," can in other contexts (with different accentuation) mean "amid the flourishing populace." Transformed by a series of rational steps, the same phrase even appears to shift from "in rich fat" (*pioni dêmôi*) by means of intermediate expressions into "he came to the land of strangers" (*allôn eksiketo dêmôn*). Formulas and formulaic expressions, Parry's proof that Homer was an oral poet similar to Balkan *guslari*, cannot themselves be defined! Furthermore, ordinary speech, although hardly metrical, is to a remarkable degree made up of set phrases hard to distinguish from Homer's formulas.

Work to define the formula proved to be a dead-end. Evidently the realities of the printed page, on which the philologist labors, are not the same as those of human speech. The elusive formula, which at first looks clear-cut then drifts away, is only behaving in the same way that "words" do in ordinary speech, whose exact definition eludes us but which we use with perfect ease. No one knows, or has good theories about, how speech works. It is an innate human faculty. Whatever the details, we cannot doubt that Homer was speaking a special language with its own vocabulary, rhythm, and units of semantic meaning, analogous to but different from ordinary speech. Somehow Homer generated his poetry within the rules, limitations, and opportunities of this special language. According to Parry's analogy, the speech of "Homeric Greek," with its many odd forms and mixture of dialects, must have been learned by absorption like an ordinary language by a young person from an older. Homeric speech had an inherent beat, a rhythm that the singer felt but did not understand in a conscious way. When the singer sings, he speaks this special language whose units are not "words" but "formulas," at least much of the time.

To say that the formulaic style limits a poet's expressiveness is therefore like saying that words limit what we can say. The rhythm drives the narrative, and words and word groups have settled down in certain places in the rhythm, which tends to break at certain places, especially in the third foot. Word groups, or formulas, fit in nicely before and after this break so that many lines, as it were, build themselves, once you have absorbed the system of word groups. Then you can talk in this language. Other Greeks can understand you, although they cannot themselves speak the language. Modern English-speakers, if they have studied Shakespeare, can follow most of it on stage, but not all, and they do not speak such English. Shakespeare is not an oral poet, but the relation between the performer's speech and that of his modern audience is similar to that between Homer and his audience.

Wolf showed how Homer could not have created the *Iliad* and the *Odyssey* because he lived in a world without writing and only writing made the poems possible. Parry showed how Homer could well have created his poems without the aid of writing, just as did the *guslari*. His formulaic style proved that Homer was an oral poet, heir to a long tradition of oral verse-making. Parry and Lord insisted on the origin of the Homeric poems through dictation, but how was this possible, if there was no writing in Homer's world?

Homer in Context: Technological and Historical Background to the Making of the First Texts

Neither Wolf nor Parry investigated the history of the technology that made Homer's texts possible – the Greek alphabet – but in recent years we have learned a good deal about its origins, the *sine qua non* of Homeric texts. In spite of their length and ambition, the *Iliad* and *Odyssey* seem to have been the first texts written in the Greek alphabet, as far as we can tell, but such extraordinary texts did not appear from nowhere or without clear historical antecedents. Although most direct information about these antecedents has been lost, we can infer a good deal from comparative study and from sparse testimonies.

No doubt the earliest texts of the *Iliad* and the *Odyssey* were encoded on papyrus, according to the predominant practice in the eastern Mediterranean on which the Greek model is based (hardly or not often on very expensive leather). Papyrus was an Egyptian invention from around 3200 BC, made from strips of a marsh plant pounded together at right angles, then cut into squares and pasted end to end. In the Ptolemaic period (323–30 BC) papyrus production was a royal monopoly and perhaps always had been. The word *papyrus* seems to mean "the thing of the [king's] house."

When we think about ancient writing, there were two spheres: the papyrus-using Egyptians and their cultural admirers on the eastern shore of the Mediterranean, and the clay-using Mesopotamians, who had the older and truly international culture. The textual (but not intellectual) tradition of the Homeric poems comes from the Egyptian sphere. Papyrus is flexible, easily stored, durable, transportable, abundant, and to some extent reusable. Clay, by contrast, was in the Bronze Age the usual medium for writing outside the papyrus-using Egypt/Levantine axis.[5] The literatures of the Sumerians and the Semitic Assyrians and Babylonians of Mesopotamia and the Indo-European Hittites of Anatolia, which go back into the third millennium BC, were all inscribed on clay tablets. The Bronze Age Cretans, too, used clay. Clay was versatile, available anywhere, cost nothing, and if you fired it would last forever, but clay is unsuitable for recording very long poems. *Gilgamesh*, by far the longest literary work to survive from 3,000 years of literate Mesopotamian culture, and of great importance to understanding the origin of the Homeric poems, is the length of about two books of the *Iliad*.

Egyptian magical texts were inscribed in narrow vertical columns, but ordinary Egyptian texts were written in lines that read from right to left arranged in broad columns, the ancestor of the modern printed page. The heirs of this writing tradition, including the Semitic Hebrews, also wrote right to left in broad columns. You held the papyrus in your left hand and unrolled it with your right, the pages also being arranged from right to left. The Egyptian sat on the ground, stretched his linen kilt taut between spread thighs, ankles crossed, and used the surface of the kilt to support the papyrus while he wrote or read. In Greece the literati did not wear kilts, but sat in chairs where they nonetheless stretched the papyrus across their knees. There were no writing desks in the ancient world.

Outside of Egypt, only the Western Semites used papyrus, those amorphous peoples who spoke a Semitic language and lived along the eastern shore of the Mediterranean and in the inland valleys (the Eastern Semites are the clay-users living in Mesopotamia). Outside Egypt where papyrus grew, papyrus was always an imported commodity, yet most documents in the eastern Mediterranean used it principally or exclusively from the earliest times.

Homer calls these seafaring papyrus-using Western Semites *Phoinikes*, "redmen," apparently because their hands were often stained from producing purple dye from shell fish, a Phoenician specialty, or *Sidonians*, "men of Sidon," a port near Byblos. The Phoenicians were never a united people, and in their disunity and relative poverty resembled the Greeks. "Phoenician" is a convenient term to distinguish the northern, coastal-dwelling Western Semites from the southern inland-dwelling Western Semites that included the Hebrews and the Canaanites, after the biblical name *Canaan* for this area, or Palestinians, after the Philistines (Indo-European Mycenaean refugees from Crete living in five towns in the Gaza strip). Geography determined the division into the coastal north and the inland south: there are several good ports in the north Levant, none in the south.

Only two good passes lead inland from the Phoenician ports in the north through the Lebanon ranges that run right along the coast. The great Bronze Age port and emporium of Ugarit lay south of one pass, ideally located to transship goods coming from inland Syria and Mesopotamia onto ships sailing to Mediterranean destinations. We will later return to the remarkable clay tablets with epic poems on them found at Ugarit, destroyed ca. 1200 BC in the general collapse of Bronze Age civilization.

The Cypriots, just 75 miles off the coast from Ugarit, were natural partners in trade and culture with Phoenicia. Cyprus was a place of transshipment for goods heading to Cilicia on the southern coast of Anatolia and to Rhodes, Euboea, and the far west. Egypt in the south was easily reached by sea. The Phoenician city of Byblos in modern Lebanon was nearly an Egyptian colony from the third millennium BC onwards and provided timber products for Egypt throughout its history, the biblical "cedars of Lebanon." Phoenician arts borrowed heavily from the Egyptians, as did the arts of Canaan, including the Hebrews.

Like the Indo-European Greeks, the Semitic Phoenicians were superb seafarers. In the Late Iron Age, under military pressure from Assyrian imperial power in northern Mesopotamia, they colonized North Africa, Spain, Sicily, and various islands in the western Mediterranean, including Sardinia, about the same time that the Greeks settled southern Italy and eastern Sicily. These *Phoinikes* turn up repeatedly in Homer's *Odyssey*, where they are greedy, knavish slavers plying their wares on the high seas. From an early time the Phoenicians shared with their Canaanite cousins a remarkable system of writing of around 22 signs. Commonly called an "alphabet," it was really an odd syllabary in which each sign stands for what we call a consonant plus an unspecified vowel. More precisely, each sign referred to a speech sound defined as an obstruction or modification of the passage of air from the mouth (the consonant), without comment on the quality of the vibration of the vocal chords (the vowel): you, the native speaker, have to fill in that sound according to context and your knowledge as a speaker of the language. In practical terms, you cannot pronounce something written in the "Phoenician alphabet" unless you are a Phoenician. Furthermore, the extreme paucity of signs, 22 or 25, enormously enhanced ambiguity; early West Semitic inscriptions, although complete and legible, are often not understood.

The "Phoenician alphabet" belonged to a family of scripts called West Semitic, which had various external forms called by scholars Ugaritic, Aramaic, Hebrew, Moabite, or Canaanite, but it was a single system of writing with local variations. The oldest example in linear form is from a sarcophagus of about 1000 BC from a King Ahiram of Byblos, but unreadable possible antecedents to West Semitic writing are found from 1800 BC, carved on rocks in remote valleys in Egypt.

Although West Semitic writing seems to be dependent in some way on Egyptian hieroglyphic writing, which also gave no information about how the vocal chords vibrated (hence is unpronounceable), its structure is unlike Egyptian writing because *all* signs in West Semitic are phonetic, whereas in Egyptian only *some* are phonetic. The origins of the West Semitic family may somehow be tied to Cretan Aegean writing, where another mostly phonetic system called Linear B, which recorded Greek, appeared at about the same time as the West Semitic writing. The Philistines in Gaza appear to be Mycenaeans from Crete, although no examples of Aegean writing have been found in Palestine.

The Western Semites so preferred Egyptian papyrus as a basis for writing that their entire literature has been lost except for the Hebrew Bible, which survived because the Jews identified their survival as a people with faithful transmission of the text. Only about 90 West Semitic inscriptions survive on hard substances from ca. 1000–300 BC in the Levant (considerably more turn up in Punic North Africa). By contrast, tens of thousands of Greek alphabetic inscriptions survive on stone and other substances. The Greeks are approaching writing in a different way.

The common but inaccurate use of the word "alphabet" to describe both the Greek alphabet and the West Semitic writing on which the Greek alphabet was based, as in "Hebrew alphabet" or "Arabic alphabet," obscures the enormous and cataclysmic historical change that took place when writing passed from the Western Semites to the Greeks. We date this moment of transference and modification of technologies by looking for the earliest Greek alphabetic inscriptions, which come from around 775 BC, then, just guessing, go back about a generation. Because after 775 BC we get a trickle, then a stream, then a river, then an ocean of inscriptions, it doesn't seem likely that the alphabet was in Greece long before our first evidence for it. The method places the invention of the Greek alphabet around 800 BC, one of the few secure dates we have in our investigation of the date of Homer. Homer must come after 800 BC because Homer is a text and texts are material things with markings on them.

The Greek alphabet and the "Phoenician" syllabary are historically related, yes, but fundamentally different in structure. The difference is best seen in the fact that you can pronounce Greek alphabetic texts without knowing the language. West Semitic writing had one kind of sign, each giving hints about the obstruction of the breath. The Greek alphabet had two separate kinds of phonetic signs. The Greek vowel signs are pronounceable by themselves, whereas the Greek consonantal signs are not pronounceable by themselves. Thus A = the sound [a], but P cannot itself be pronounced (even if we might say [puh] if someone asked us). In West Semitic, by contrast, P would = [pa], [pu], [po] or some other combination and a native speaker would know which. The invention of the Greek alphabet on the basis of the Phoenician syllabary depended, first, on the division of the signs into two different kinds and, second, on the spelling rule that one of the five vocalic signs must always notate every consonantal sign. BCKUP, the spelling preferred by Microsoft Word, is therefore a mixture of West Semitic and Greek practice, but such common usages as CMDR (= commander), painted on US war planes, are a return to ancient West Semitic practice. If you speak English, you guess it's "commander" but otherwise you're out of luck. Such license is never allowed in ancient Greek orthography, where the spelling rule that you must have both kinds of signs is inviolable.

Four hundred years earlier than the sarcophagus of Ahiram come our very earliest certain examples of West Semitic writing, but written in a nonlinear script, ca. 1400, on clay tablets from Ugarit, the Bronze Age emporium destroyed ca. 1200 BC. The signs are made up of wedges pushed into clay in the way that wedges make up the otherwise un-related "cuneiform" writing of Mesopotamia. This "Ugaritic alphabet" was apparently a free invention by someone used to writing with wedges on clay and survives only in Ugarit and its near environs. Because these odd Ugaritic texts were impressed in clay in imitation of Mesopotamian practice instead of on the usual papyrus, they survived the sack of the city and we can read them today.

Fifteen tablets preserve the story about the triumph of the storm god Baal ("lord") over his enemies Yamm ("sea") and Mot ("death"), the son of El ("god"). We learn of Baal's imprisonment in the underworld, whence his sister/wife Anat freed him, and about Baal's victorious king-ship over gods and men. Other tablets record legends close to the sort of histories we find in the Bible, based on similar semi-legendary accounts of historical figures.

A unique statement appended to the end of the Baal tablets reports that they were taken down by one Ilimilku from Shubani as dictated by the chief priest Atanu-Purliani. For their efforts, both were supported by Niqmadu II, king of Ugarit, who reigned from 1375–1345 BC. The colophon draws a clear distinction between the composer of the mythical text, Atanu-Purliani, and its recorder, Ilimilku, a procedure for which there is no clear example in any earlier tradition of writing. The earliest attested use of West Semitic writing, the "cuneiform alphabet," the direct ancestor of the Greek alphabet, is therefore seemingly to take down a literary text by dictation.

Even so, Jeremiah dictated to his scribe Baruch (Jeremiah 36.18), and perhaps all the early texts of what became the Old Testament are the result of dictation. The odd focus on purely phonetic but unpronounceable elements in West Semitic writing, which made it unlearnable except by someone who spoke the language, may well reflect this writing's origin in the practice of dictation as a means of composition. The composer speaks, and the scribe represents the sounds as best he can. In this way you can write anything you can say, so long as there is enough context for a literate speaker to reconstruct the message. If you applied the West Semitic system to write down in this way the first line of the *Iliad*, and separated the words by dots as the Phoenicians did, it might look something like

MNN•D•T•PLD•KLS

for the Greek alphabetic

MENIN AEIDE THEA PELEIADEO AKHILEOS.

Whereas the West Semitic system of writing worked after a fashion for West Semitic languages, whose words are built around an unvarying consonantal skeleton, it did not work for Greek verse, filled with contiguous vowel sounds that establish the verse's rhythm. To judge from very early inscriptional finds in hexametric verse, the Greek alphabet was from the beginning used for just this purpose. Perhaps a bilingual Semite, heir to an ancient tradition of taking down poetry by dictation, tried his hand at taking down Greek song. Making technical alterations to the West Semitic Writing to accommodate the very different phonology of Greek speech, he established two kinds of signs and the inviolable spelling rule that made Homer's text possible. He invented the first true alphabet, the first writing that can be pronounced by someone who is not a speaker of that language, a system now used over virtually the entire planet.

Oral Song Becomes Text

Parry was interested in oral poetry as a living, breathing tradition, but Homer's poems are not oral poems; they are texts, the philologist's Homer. An oral poem is a public event, a performance before an audience, usually small, where there is music, facial expression, gesture, emphasis, and spontaneous adaptation to the mood of the audience. Homer himself gives us a vivid picture of the oral poet, the *aoidos*, and his oral song in the *Odyssey*, where a singer named Phemius (= "famous one") entertains the suitors in the house of Odysseus, and another singer Demodocus (= "pleasing to the people") holds in rapt attention the Phaeacian court, where Odysseus tells of his strange journey. The *aoidos* is a commanding presence in the court and provides life with a special richness and meaning:

> For myself I declare that there is no greater fulfillment of delight than when joy possesses a whole people, and banqueters in the halls listen to an *aoidos* as they sit all in order, and beside them tables are laden with bread and meat, and the cup-bearer draws wine from the bowl and carries it around and pours it in the cups. This seems to my mind the fairest thing there is. (*Od.* 9.5–11)

Such men held a special place in Greek society, analogous to religious leaders in other ancient societies, whom according to an extraordinary development in Greece the *aoidoi* replaced. The *aoidoi*, not the priests, defined moral values in Greek society.

A text, by contrast to oral song, is a physical object with marks on it capable of interpretation, if you are clever. A text allows the reconstruction of a phonetic version of the signs intelligible to someone who speaks Greek, but not similar even theoretically to any song that any poet ever sang. Specialists called *rhapsodes* memorized these texts and while holding a staff delivered them in a histrionic fashion at public gatherings, especially at the Athenian festival of the Panathenaea reformed by Pisistratus in the sixth century BC. *Rhapsode* probably means "staff-singer," but the Greeks falsely etymologized it to mean "stitcher of song." *Rhapsodes* are not descended from the *aoidoi* who generated their song afresh with each performance, but from the inventor of the Greek alphabet, whose spelling rule allowed an approximate notation of the actual sounds of Greek verse. *Rhapsodes*, unlike *aoidoi*, could read and write and like proto-professors prided themselves on their ability to explicate a text, above all Homer's text. Plato snidely mocks such pretensions in his dialogue *Ion* from the fourth century BC. Plato does not trust men like Ion, who take pride in scholastic mastery of a text and think that truth resides therein:

> *Socrates:* I often envy the profession of a rhapsode, Ion, for you always wear fine clothes. Looking as beautiful as possible is part of your art. Furthermore you are obligated to be constantly in the company of many good poets, especially Homer, best and most divine of poets. To understand him and not merely learn his words by rote memorization is a thing greatly to be envied. And no man can be a rhapsode who does not understand the poet's meaning, for the rhapsode should interpret the mind of the poet to his listeners. But how can he interpret him well unless he knows what the poet means? All this is greatly to be envied.
>
> *Ion:* Very true, Socrates. Interpretation has surely been the most laborious part of my art, and I believe myself able to speak about Homer better than any man. Neither Metrodorus of Lampsacus nor Stesimbrotus of Thasos nor Glaucon nor any one else who ever lived had as good ideas about Homer as I have, or as many. (Plato, *Ion*, 530b–d)

Unlike the oral poet, who is an entertainer, the *rhapsode* is also a proto-scholar. He not only recites, but he explicates, using the text as a basis for teaching (teaching what? Plato goes on to wonder).

It is important not to confuse "oral poem," what an *aoidos* sings, with Homer's text, which an *aoidos* dictated and a *rhapsode* memorizes and recites. Getting these two mixed up has led to much confusion in modern Homeric studies, so that some think that Homer sang something similar to our texts of the *Iliad* and *Odyssey* throughout his career, or that the "same poems" were sung by other poets during their own careers. It would then be possible for different people in different places at different times to have written down the *Iliad* or the *Odyssey*, as we know that the medieval French *Chanson de Roland* was taken down in different versions from different singers. According to the Parry/Lord model, however, our *Iliad* and *Odyssey* are unique versions that came into being at a single time when, under unusual circumstances, a poet dictated his song to an amanuensis.

We can only speculate about earlier or later forms of these songs, but can be sure that they bore scant resemblance to our *Iliad* and *Odyssey*.

Because of their enormous length (about 16,000 lines for the *Iliad* and 12,000 lines for the *Odyssey*) these poems remain a transcendent mystery in the history of literature. The average length of an oral song, according to Parry's studies and modern field studies, runs to about 800 lines, roughly the length of a single book of the *Iliad*. As we will see in part two of this book, the poems are made up of just such shorter elements that may in some form have stood alone. The oral singer is limited by the attention-span of his audience and by his own powers of voice and bearing. What can such long poems have been for? Not for readers who read for edification or pleasure, because there can have been none when Homer lived. There is no writing in Homer's world and there are no poets who pore over papyri. Yet the poems seem to have existed in writing from the very dawn of alphabetic literacy in the eighth century BC.

No doubt as a professional *aoidos* the historical Homer sang the anger of Achilles and the homecoming of Odysseus many times, but our textual versions are determined by the conditions under which the stories were transferred from the invisible and ephemeral realm of oral song into the visible and material realm of a written text. Their extraordinary length and manifest desire, annoying to a modern reader, constantly to prolong the narrative divorces them as works of entertainment from real songs sung in real time to real audiences. The form and length of the poems depend on the unique circumstances of the creation of the texts. In the experience of Parry and Lord, the very process of dictation encouraged a longer and more elaborate poem. Freed from the challenge and restraints of live performance, the *guslar* could spin out the tale as he chose. As we have seen, Parry prodded one singer, his favorite, into dictating a song as long as the *Odyssey*. There is no writing in Homer, yet he was written down, as Wolf complained 200 years ago.

The Date of Homer's Texts

Although most handbooks call Homer an Ionian poet, who lived and worked in Asia Minor, he may have worked on the long island of Euboea that hugs the east coast of mainland Greece. Certain technical features of his dialect may mark it as West Ionian, as opposed to the East Ionian of the Asia Minor coast. According to recent archeological finds on Euboea at Lefkandi, a modern name for an ancient settlement at the edge of the much-contested Lelantine Plain that separates the rival Euboean towns of Chalcis and Eretria, Euboeans were the most advanced and wealthiest of all Greek communities during the Greek Dark Ages ca. 1100–800 BC. Objects of Egyptian and Near Eastern origin in graves from this period prove that the Euboeans alone of mainland Greeks maintained contact, directly or through middlemen, with Cyprus and the Levantine coast and even Egypt. Within an enormous, long, narrow structure with an apse at one end, built around 1000 BC, unparalleled anywhere in Greece, was an extraordinary warrior's cremation burial, along with sacrificed horses and gold ornaments in the accompanying inhumation burial of a woman. In just such an environment we imagine the *aoidoi* to have plied their trade.

The Euboeans were the earliest and most aggressive of Greek colonizers, and the *Odyssey* is a poem tailor-made to fit their historical experience in the western Mediterranean in the "Wild West" days of the late ninth and early eighth centuries BC. By the second quarter of the eighth century BC they had permanent posts in southern Italy, including one at Cumae on the Bay of Naples, so important to Vergil's story of migration to Italy. At the same time Euboeans maintained permanent posts in northern Syria near the Orontes estuary, not far from the Bronze Age emporium of Ugarit, home to West Semitic traditions of culture and writing. The oldest example of Greek alphabetic writing appears to be part of a name, EULIN, recently discovered on a clay pot found, to everyone's astonishment, in Latium in Italy, dated by stratigraphy to ca. 775 BC. Latium is near Euboean Cumae on the Bay of Naples and the Euboean settlement on Ischia in the bay, where other very early pieces of writing are found. Sherds with pieces of names are found from about the same early date of 775–750 BC on Euboea itself.

As we have seen, the Greek alphabet's obsession with phonetic representation (so unlike earlier systems of writing) is internal evidence that it was invented to notate hexametric verse, perhaps even the *Iliad* and the *Odyssey*. Certainly its Phoenician model was incapable of notating such Homeric words as *aaatos*, "decisive," which in Phoenician script would be written *ts*! Although vowel clusters are common in Greek, such extravagant examples are found only in verse, where the sequence of vocalic sounds assists the formation of the complex rhythm. In any event you do not need phonetic verisimilitude to make a written record of just any Greek, as proven by the Linear B script, which provides only a rough approx-imation of the sound of any spoken word.

Our earliest inscriptions support the theory that the desire to record hexametric verse inspired the invention of the Greek alphabet. Still probably the oldest "long inscription" of more than a few letters was found

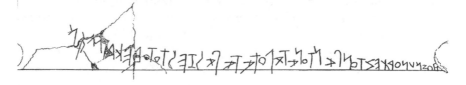

Figure 2   The Dipylon Vase inscription (from Powell 1991: fig. 58) 23

in 1871 in Athens, called the Dipylon Vase inscription (see figure 2). The inscription has been scratched with a sharp object ripping through the glaze of a pot made in a shop just outside the Dipylon Gate in Athens ca. 740 BC. Reading from right to left, it preserves a perfect dactylic hexameter followed by some signs of unclear meaning, perhaps partly a garbled portion of an abecedary (the signs of the alphabet in a row).

ΗΟΣΝΥΝΟΡΧΕΣΤΟΝΠΑΝΤΟΝΑΤΑΛΟΤΑΤΑΠΑΙΖΕΙΤΟΤΟΔΕΚ{Μ} Μ{Ν?}Ν

Whoever of all the dancers now dances most gracefully . . .

Another "long inscription" was found on Euboean Ischia in the Bay of Naples on a Rhodian drinking cup, made ca. 740 BC, about the same time as the Dipylon Vase inscription. Called the Cup of Nestor inscription, the first line seems to be prose, but the second and third are again dactylic hexameters. In translation:

> I am the cup of Nestor, a joy to drink from.
> Whoever drinks from this cup, straightway that man
> The desire of beautiful-crowned Aphrodite will seize.

The find excited wide attention because the cup appears to refer to the cup of Nestor described in Book 11 of the *Iliad* (632–5), when Patroclus comes to Nestor's tent to ask about a wounded companion:

> The maid first drew before the two a fine table with feet of well-polished lapis and set on it a bronze basket and with it an onion, a relish for their drink, and pale honey and ground meal of sacred barley and beside them a beautiful cup that the old man brought from home, studded with bosses of gold; there were four handles on it and about each two doves were

feeding, while below were two supports. Another man could scarce have lifted that cup from the table when full, but old Nestor raised it easily. (*Il.* 11.628–37)

In one of the shaft graves at Mycenae Heinrich Schliemann found a cup that resembles Homer's description, suggesting that the cup, like the boar's tusk helmet, may be a Mycenaean heirloom. If the "cup of Nestor" of the inscription is the same as that in *Iliad* 11, the *Iliad* must have existed before the inscription was made around 740 BC. The inscription would then be a "time before which" (*terminus ante quem*) for the composition of the *Iliad*. Some think, however, that the cup of Nestor was a traditional motif on the lips of many poets, although the only cup of Nestor we know anything about is the one described by Homer.

The Greek alphabet was therefore used from the earliest times to notate epic verse. Because Homer's texts cannot predate the Greek alphabet, and because no object described in the Homeric poems post-dates 700 BC, and because the Cup of Nestor Inscription may refer to the *Iliad*, and because of the social and historical conditions reflected in the poems (see chapter 2), the first texts of Homer must belong to the eighth century BC. When in the eighth century? Many scholars place him in the second half, to give the alphabet a chance to "ripen" and become sophisticated enough to fashion our texts. But the alphabet did not begin as a primitive device that became more sophisticated in time. The Greek alphabet appeared within a tradition of taking down texts by dictation perhaps 1,000 years old in the days of Homer. Placing Homer in the second half of the eighth century does not adequately take account of Homer's ignorance of the tradition of writing that made his texts possible, which will place him close to its invention around 800 BC. Greek legend said that a man named Palamedes invented the Greek alphabet, and maybe he did. In myth, Palamedes was a Euboean who lived in Nauplius, "ship-town" (not the Nauplion in the Peloponnesus). Because legends preserve real names, Palamedes may be the name of Homer's amanuensis, although we cannot prove it.

Someone of great wealth and power stood behind the creation of these texts. The cost of the papyrus alone was great, and the whole project was an insane ambition, as sometimes happens at the beginning of a new technology. For example, the most ambitious stone temple complex in Egypt, surrounding the step-pyramid of King Djoser ca. 2600 BC, is also the earliest. The dictating of the poems was laborious and expensive, but the Euboeans had the means and through their

Eastern contacts now the technology of writing. It is likely that the *Iliad* and the *Odyssey*, as well as the poems of Hesiod from nearby Boeotia, were written down on the island of Euboea and were first in the possession of Euboeans.

What can have been our Palamedes' motives for fashioning texts of unprecedented length and complexity? What did our scribe, who had the backing of wealth and an unknown purpose, do with the texts once he had them? If he was also the inventor of the alphabet, he was the only man in the world able to read the first texts, until others learned the secrets of his method. We know that Homer's texts were the basis of Greek education by the sixth century BC; plausibly they were the basis for Greek education from the moment of the alphabet's invention.

2

The Historian's Homer

The philologist wants to know the origin of the first text of the *Iliad* and the *Odyssey* (but by no means the beginning of the tradition embodied in those texts, which must be very old). The historian shares the philologist's keen interest in the date when the epics came into being, but wishes then to extract from Homer's texts as much information as possible about how people lived then and what they thought. Homer sang the *Iliad* and *Odyssey* and someone created a text from his song. But how much of this long-ago world depends on poetic fancy and how much reflects a real world in which a real poet once lived? Here is the historian's challenge.

Homer and the Bronze Age

Homer's relationship to the Bronze Age remains a persistent problem. Archeological research has revealed the rich and powerful world of the Mycenaean Greeks that flourished ca. 1600–1150 BC and collapsed in a general conflagration in the Balkans, the Aegean Sea, and Anatolia (but not in the Near East). The Trojan War, if there was a Trojan War, must have taken place in the Bronze Age. Heinrich Schliemann (1822–90), who discovered the Greek Bronze Age when he excavated Troy in Asia Minor and Mycenae on the Greek mainland in the late nineteenth century, appeared to prove that Homer's stories must somehow be based in fact, in history. After all, Mycenae and Troy were real places that really were burned down. Homer was describing the Bronze Age, Schliemann thought, and until recently many have agreed. The powerful, even astonishing, walls of what Homer aptly calls "well-girt Troy" and the overtly military style of the Mycenaean citadels and the exquisite armor found in Mycenaean graves, including a gold death-mask that Schliemann thought belonged to Agamemnon, king of Mycenae, rich in gold, agreed with Homer's general descriptions of wealthy Greeks with a taste for aggression and wealthy Trojans in a position to resist it. The citadel at Mycenae well accorded with the power of Agamemnon as described by Homer; in the Classical Period, by contrast, Mycenae was a miserable village. The later work of Parry/Lord appeared to validate the equation Homer's world = Mycenaean Greece because it explained how through oral tradition Homer could inherit good knowledge of what happened 400 years earlier.

The more we learned about the Greek Bronze Age, however, the greater appeared the discrepancy between it and Homer's world. Homer knows nothing about the enormous Mycenaean "beehive" or *tholos* tombs, a sort of underground conical vault sometimes of huge dimensions, visited today by millions of tourists every year outside the walls of Mycenae. In Homer's poems, bodies are always cremated, whereas in the Bronze Age they were interred. Homer knows nothing of the palace bureaucracies supported by the syllabic writing we call Linear B, engraved by professional scribes on clay tablets. Homer's picture of independent warrior chieftains who live, like Odysseus, in rectangular pitched-roof halls with no decoration and packed earth floors poorly agrees with the regulated monarchies of Bronze Age Mycenae, Cnossus, Pylos, and Thebes, where kings lived in square flat-roofed halls with stone floors and elaborate fresco decorations on the walls, whence they presided over an elaborate and hierarchical economic machine.

A once long list of Bronze Age elements claimed for the *Iliad* and the *Odyssey* has shrunk to a few items. There is the Trojan War itself – assuming that some historical incident must have inspired stories about it. Weapons are always made of bronze, although Homer describes everyday tools as made of iron. There is the helmet made of boars' tusks sewn to a felt cap mentioned in Book 10 of the *Iliad*, the "Song of Dolon" (10. 260–71). Illustrations of just such odd helmets appear on frescoes at Pylos ca. 1200 BC in the southwest Peloponnesus and, astonishingly, on papyri from the capital of the Egyptian heretic pharaoh Akhenaten (ca. 1367–1350 BC). Parts of such helmets are found in Mycenaean graves from the sixteenth to eleventh centuries BC, but they are never illustrated after around 1200 BC, when they seem to have gone out of style. In fact Homer calls the helmet an heirloom, something from an earlier age, and even gives its pedigree; even in Homer it is an antique.

Most shields in Homer are round, but several times Homer describes a shield "like a wall," which Ajax carries (e.g., *Il.* 7.219). Hector's shield is usually round, but once it is so large that it "bangs against his ankles and neck" (*Il.* 6.117–18), as if it too were "like a wall." Homer seems to confuse two kinds of shield, the round shield common already toward the end of the Late Bronze Age, and another earlier one similar to the high, broad shields pictured on daggers from the shaft graves at Mycenae, ca. 1600 BC. The Cretans from an early time had used tall body-shields in the shape of a figure of eight made of oxhide stretched over a wooden frame. The Mycenaean Greeks copied this style of shield from them, and Homer seems to know something about it.

A similar confusion between old and new appears in Homer's descriptions of fighting with spears. According to artistic representations, fighters in the Bronze Age used a single, thrusting spear, sometimes very long. All figural illustrations disappear from Greek art around 1150 BC, but when warriors again appear in Geometric art of the eighth century BC they now carry two spears, shorter and lighter. These must be the javelins that Homeric warriors throw at one another. Achilles, by contrast, greatest warrior of all, still fights with a single huge spear, yet this he throws, as if it were a javelin (*Il.* 22.273)!

There are evidently strata in such descriptions, as if a few things from earlier times, from the Bronze Age itself, have got frozen in the highly stylized oral-formulaic language of the *aoidoi.* Several metrical irregularities in the vulgate text are explicable on a reconstruction of forms that may have been current in the Bronze Age. The song tradition must therefore go back to the Late Bronze Age, and maybe earlier. Homer has no sense of history. Oral song speaks to the concerns and assumptions of contemporaries, who have no sense of history either. If you are an *aoidos,* it is important to be up with the times, to know the latest song. Telemachus, Odysseus' son, snaps to his mother Penelope, who complains about Phemius' song about the Trojan War:

My mother, why do you oppose letting the good minstrel give pleasure any way he chooses? It is not *aoidoi* that are to blame, but Zeus I think is to blame, who gives to men that live by labor to each as he wishes. No one can be angry if he sings of the evil doom of the Danaans, for men praise that song the most which comes newest to their ears. (*Od.* 1.346–52)

Homer's World and the Classical Polis

Most scholars now agree that Homer's world, while embodying artifacts from earlier times, from the Bronze Age and the Iron Age, is mostly the world of his own day, the eighth century BC, a period now called the Greek Renaissance. Truly in the eighth century BC a new world was being born in Hellas from the detritus of the Mycenaean civilization that had collapsed 300 years before. If we can trust Homer's testimony, the *polis*, usually translated "city-state," the characteristic manner of political organization in the Classical Period, was even then beginning to come into being.

The classical *polis* was a development of the *oikos* or "household" as an economic unit with a structure of authority. Homer well describes the *oikos* of Odysseus on Ithaca, where the master of the house has absolute authority even to kill members of his household or those who threaten it. He owns surrounding lands and orchards and herds by which he supports his family and slaves. Telemachus, seeking support outside the *oikos* for violations within it, calls an assembly of neighboring *oikoi*, the first in 20 years (*Od.* 2.26–7), to complain about the suitors, but the assembly lacks the power to act. From such assemblies will later grow the full-blown legislative bodies of the classical *polis*.

The classical *polis* grew through consolidation, by whatever means, of many *oikoi* into a single unit. A *polis* included the free people living within a certain geographical area, both those within a city with its walls, buildings, and places of meeting, and those who lived in the outlying countryside, with its farms, slaves, and livestock. The *polis* is a kind of miniature state that unifies its diverse members through common goals and myths and a place of assembly (*agora*) for all adult males to meet and make decisions affecting the group, not just the elite such as Odysseus, Achilles, and Agamemnon.

A *polis* is focused on a god or gods who embody its strength and spirit and sponsor its success. The gods are ritually flattered in having their own precincts or temples. There are already such freestanding temples in the *Iliad*, where Homer describes the Trojan queen at the head of a procession to place a robe on the knees of Athena (*Il.* 6.297). The image is within a temple served by a priestess with a key, the only clear reference in the poems to a cult practice common in the classical *polis*. The centerpiece of the Panathenaic Festival in Athens was the giving of a new robe to Athena's statue in the Parthenon. In no sense is Troy, ruled by a hereditary king, a Greek *polis*, and the giving of the robe may depend on an Eastern literary exemplar. For 2,000 years before Homer, Mesopotamians and Egyptians had paid daily attention to, and regularly changed the clothes of, statues in shrines. Still, the detail nicely accords with the earliest temples to appear in Greece, in the early eighth century BC (from Perachora near Corinth and on the island of Samos).

There are other hints in Homer that the *polis* is coming into being. When Hector declares that "he has no dishonor who dies fighting for his country, for then his wife shall be saved, and his children, and his houses and buildings shall not be damaged" (*Il.* 15.496–8), he declares loyalty to a public sphere as well as a private one. In the *Odyssey*, Alcinous, king of the Phaeacians, rules over a walled city built on a peninsula, where there are no temples, but special places set aside for the gods.

The sure sign of the evolved *polis* was the hoplite line, or *phalanx*, when the citizens stood side by side in a rigorous formation of rows many ranks deep. With his left hand, the warrior protected his neighbor's right flank while presenting his single thrusting spear to the enemy, who stood in a similar formation. Several times Homer refers to a *phalanx* of fighters (e.g., *Il.* 6.6, 11.90), the same word used for the formation of hoplite fighters in the classical *polis*, but he cannot mean the same thing. In the classical *phalanx* the hoplite warrior does not fight for himself, but for the protection of the man beside him and the glory of the *polis* that the formation of the *phalanx* represents. The whole spirit of the *polis* was embodied in the classical *phalanx*. In Homeric fighting, by contrast, the individual hero stands before the crowd, eager to win acclamation and personal glory, although sometimes the assembled fighters fall into dense formations.

The shift between the glory-hungry heroes of Homer's Trojan War and the glory-hungry *polis* of the Classical Period is radical, and the hoplite *phalanx* is the sign that we have crossed the divide. We can probably date this shift to the early seventh century BC, to judge from shields dedicated at the shrine of Zeus at Olympia, a nice accord with other evidence that Homer belongs in the eighth century BC. Earlier shields, like those in Homer, were carried by a strap across the shoulder, a *telamon*, but the hoplite fighter carried his small round shield by means of a loop affixed in the center of the shield through which he passed his arm to grip a fixture at the edge of the shield. Thus the hoplite fighter could use his shield as a weapon in close encounter. We cannot trace the evolution of the hoplite line as such and it may have been an invention that appeared suddenly at one time.[6] Against

Homeric-style fighters, an organized line would be devastating, and once someone tried it, other communities would follow or perish.

Homer and the Age of Colonial Expansion

The *Iliad* is a traditional tale about heroic behavior, hence more stylized than the *Odyssey* and less interested in Homer's contemporary world. The *Odyssey*, by contrast, with its theme of travel to distant lands, gives a vivid picture of an exciting and dangerous world inspired by contemporary Euboean adventure in the far west in the eighth century BC. In this dangerous world men sail for long distances on open boats, encounter storms and other more fantastic dangers, and sometimes return home laden with booty. In the following passage, in a "lying tale" that Odysseus tells to the swineherd Eumaeus when he returns to Ithaca, he describes the restless, aggressive spirit that was changing the political and economic structure of peoples living around the Mediterranean Sea during the Greek Renaissance of the eighth century BC:

> Ares and Athena gave me courage, and strength that breaks the ranks of men; and whenever I picked the best warriors for an ambush, sowing the seeds of evil for the enemy, never did my proud spirit fear death, but always I was first to leap forth and kill with my spear whoever of the foe gave way in flight before me. Such a man I was in war, but labor in the field was not to my liking, nor the care of a household, which rears fine children. Oared ships were ever dear to me and wars and polished spears and arrows – grievous things, at which others shudder. (*Od*. 14.216–26)

A sailor of wide experience, he goes on to explain how he attacked even Egypt, was captured, then turned over to Phoenicians who planned to enslave him. The Phoenicians sailed from somewhere in the Levant and drove before the wind toward Libya, but are storm-wrecked on southern Crete. Odysseus improbably lands in Thresprotia, a territory far to the north of Crete on the mainland opposite Ithaca.

At the end of the Iron Age in the late ninth and early eighth centuries BC the Phoenicians were in fact ethnic and cultural antagonists to the Greeks, or lived with them cheek by jowl as both groups exploited the mineral and other wealth of Africa, Sicily, Sardinia, Italy, Spain, and France. Phoenicians built the city of Kition in southern Cyprus some time in the ninth century BC in close proximity to the Greek city of Salamis that lay to the northeast. Phoenicians were living at Kommos on the south coast of Crete from the mid-ninth century BC too – perhaps on the same route that Odysseus describes in his false tale. In the eighth century BC they built a tripartite stone temple at Kommos in the Semitic Levantine style. Very early Phoenician inscriptions, perhaps from the late ninth century BC, are found on Sardinia. Phoenician jewelers were living near Cnossus around 900 BC, to judge from finds. From the archeological evidence, the Phoenician expansion began in the early ninth century BC, no doubt in response to pressure by the powerful Assyrians under Ashurnasirpal II (ruled 883–859 BC), who at this time defeated the Aramaeans of north Syria (Aram = Damascus), then marched via Carchemish on the Euphrates to the Mediterranean and occupied the Levantine ports.

Homer's descriptions of Phoenician/Greek rivalry and hostility, yet occasional intimacy (Eumaeus' nurse was a Phoenician woman), accords closely with the archeological evidence that Phoenicians and Greeks lived together on the island of Ischia in the Bay of Naples in the eighth century BC. Of course, the Greeks are adapting their writing from that of the Phoenicians. Whereas we cannot follow Odysseus' famous and fantastic wanderings on a map, already in Hesiod's *Theogony* Circe's residence is placed on an island off the Italian coast (*Theogony* 1015–16) and the dangerous Straits of Messina between Sicily and Italy seem to stand behind the mythical Scylla and Charybdis, according to Thucydides (4.24). Thucydides (1.25) also identifies Phaeacia with Corcyra, and Ithaca is the jumping off place for travel from East to West.

Odysseus has the sure evaluating eye of the experienced colonist at a time when the earliest Greek colonies are about to spring up in southern Italy and Sicily. The earliest colony was on Ischia ca. 775 BC, and most other western colonies followed in the last third of the eighth century BC. The bestial Cyclopes are like the foreign peoples who lack Greek crafts, skills, and imagination, monstrous in their way of life as they are monstrous in appearance. Of the island that lies across from the Cyclops' cave, Homer says:

> Now there is a level island that stretches at an angle outside the harbor, neither close to the shore of the land of the Cyclopes, nor yet far off, a wooded isle. There live wild goats beyond counting, for the tread of men does not scare them away, nor do hunters come there, who endure labors in the woodland as they course over mountain peaks. Neither do flocks

dwell there, nor is the land ploughed, but unsown and untilled all the
days it knows nothing of men, but feeds the bleating goats. For the
Cyclopes have at hand no ships with vermilion cheeks, nor are there ship
builders in their land who might build them well-benched ships that
would perform all their needs in passing to the cities of other people as
men often cross the sea in ships to visit one another – craftsmen who
would have made of this isle also a fair settlement. For the island is in no
way poor, but would bear all things in season. In it are meadows by the
shores of the gray sea, well-watered meadows and soft, where vines would
never fail, and in it level plow land whence they might reap from season
to season deep harvests, so rich is the soil beneath, and in it, too, is a
harbor giving safe anchorage, where there is no need of moorings, either to
throw out anchor-stones or to make fast stern-cables, but one may beach
one's ship and wait until the sailors' minds bid them put out, and the
breezes blow fair. (*Od.* 9.116–39)

Odysseus may here have the eye of a man of colonial enterprise, but
Odysseus' fictional character in the story he tells to Eumaeus is a man
of violence, who rejects home and family. He is a pirate, a killer, and a
thief, who becomes wealthy through depredation, hence respected in his
Cretan home where no moral opprobrium attaches to his behavior. Not
only in the general climate of the *Odyssey* do we seem to perceive the
realia of Greek life in the eighth century BC, but also in the cut-throat
behavior of its relentless, brave-hearted men.

Homer and Art

Homer's fascination with objects of art that are vivid and lifelike provides a good example of the problems we face in trying to establish a
relationship between a real historical world and the story Homer tells.
He must be inspired by objects he has seen, but through poetic invention has transformed them into something new. In Book 18 of the *Iliad*
Homer describes Hephaestus crafting a shield for Achilles (see cover
photo). It is a beautiful, extraordinary object, a living thing. The narrative on the shield is not, however, set in the heroic age where Homer's
own story plays out, where gods converse with men, but in an everyday
world that must be Homer's own.

    On the shield are two cities, one at peace and one at war. In the city
at peace is a wedding and the public resolution of a homicide, a pre-*polis*

post-Bronze Age world in which kings do not adjudicate, as elsewhere in Homer, nor courts, as in the classical *polis*, but "judges," men acclaimed for wisdom and fairness:

> But the people were gathered in the place of assembly, for a conflict had arisen, and two men were in strife about the blood-price of a man who was killed. The one declared that he had paid all, proclaiming his cause to the people, but the other refused to accept it, and each hoped to win the dispute on the word of a referee. The people were cheering both sides, showing favor to this side and that. Heralds held back the people, and the elders sat on polished stones in the sacred circle, holding in their hands the staffs of the loud-voiced heralds. With these they would spring up and give judgment, each in turn. In the midst lay two talents of gold to be given to him who among them should utter the most righteous judgment. (*Il.* 18.497–508)

In the city at war, an army prepares a siege from one side while from the other an ambush from the city leads to an all-out battle. There is Strife and Tumult and Fate, but no Apollo or Ares or Hera. There are also scenes of plowing, harvesting, feasting, the tending of grapes, herds and lions that attack them, and a dancing floor.

Judging from the tools Hephaestus uses, the designs in Achilles' shield were worked in repoussé, a technique of hammering and pressing designs in relief, not the Mycenaean metalwork of exquisite inlay. A half-dozen surviving Phoenician metal bowls and dedicatory shields from the eighth and seventh centuries BC are similarly worked in repoussé. They show elaborate scenes in an Egyptianizing style of dance and feasting and kings sitting on thrones. There are also cities under siege and hunts. Homer and his audience must have seen objects like these, found in Nimrud in Assyria, on Crete, on Cyprus, and in Italy.

Homer never describes mythical events on objects of art, but by the end of the first quarter of the seventh century, around 675 BC, Greek artists begin to make pictures of Greek myths. Almost simultaneously on the Aegean islands of Samos and Mykonos and from Etruscan Caere in Italy are found pictures of a team of men blinding a one-eyed giant, one of the oldest certain artistic representations of a Greek myth. The representation of myth in art is a radical shift in the history of art. Narrative art in pictures is familiar to us because of the Greek tradition, but without good analogues in earlier Near Eastern and Egyptian art, which was almost entirely political, commemorative, decorative, or magical. Although Mesopotamians made pictures of monsters, mostly on tiny seals, to which Greek art owes a good deal, we are never sure of the names of these monsters or their deeds. By contrast, all agree that several men blinding a huge man with a stake represents the story of Odysseus blinding Polyphemus.

Had the Polyphemus artists of ca. 675 BC in some way been exposed to the text of Homer's *Odyssey*, presumably through rhapsodic presentation? It is hard to explain otherwise why no one ever made a picture of a team of men blinding a one-eyed giant until then, when artists from one end of the Mediterranean to the other suddenly did so, unless they were all subject to the same stimulus. As in the case of the Cup of Nestor, to which the Ischia inscription refers, the only evidence we have for the existence in ancient Greece of the Polyphemus story is Homer's poem, and it is plausible that copies of *Odyssey* Book 9, excerpted from the *Odyssey*, did in fact circulate independently in the early seventh century among Greek travelers. The poem has inspired the pictures.

After 675 BC and the Polyphemus pictures, "mythic" representations begin to flood through Greek art. Most myths illustrated in Greek art in the seventh and sixth centuries BC are not, however, taken from the *Iliad* and the *Odyssey*, but from epic poems now lost. These poems are called the Cyclic Poems because they appeared to be composed "in a circle" around the *Iliad* and the *Odyssey*, filling out what came before and after the Trojan War. Texts of the Cyclic Poems were no doubt better known than the *Iliad* and the *Odyssey* because they were far shorter, thus more portable, easier to store, less expensive to reproduce, and easier to recite. Texts, reproducible and memorizable, of once oral poems were spreading the knowledge of Greek epic into every corner of Greek society. The spread of such texts must stand behind the revolutionary change of subject matter in Greek art in the seventh century BC. The province of the *aoidos*, with his storehouse of myth, was the hall of the numerically few rich and powerful; *rhapsodes* declaimed before the people whenever they got the chance.

Homer and the Near East

Homer's poems are regarded as the beginning of classical Greek civilization, the *fons et origo* of Western culture. As the first texts in the Greek alphabet, which became the basis for Greek and Roman education, they are just that. On the other hand, as the Greek alphabet was based on a preexisting all-phonetic writing 1,000 years old in the days of Homer, so were Homer's stories, and much of his imaginative world, taken from earlier Eastern and especially Semitic peoples. Many are surprised that the basic stories of the *Iliad* and the *Odyssey* are not Greek in origin. In recent decades we have learned how Homer is part of a cultural continuum traceable to the fourth millennium BC in the ancient Near East. We must understand Homer in the context of the greater and earlier world beyond.

Our best source of information about pre-Greek legend is in the Akkadian epic *Gilgamesh*, which survives in its most complete version on 12 tablets found at the Assyrian capital of Nineveh destroyed in 612 BC by a coalition of Babylonians and Persians. But the poem is much older; pieces of it have been found as early as the third millennium written in the Sumerian language in cuneiform script. Other portions turned up in the Indo-European Hittite capital of Hattusas, destroyed ca. 1200 BC, and in other scattered settlements around the Near East. Such texts are never dictated transcriptions of oral songs, however, but scribal compositions created in the scribal workshops to impress, amuse, and instruct other scribes.

The story of Gilgamesh, whose close friend Enkidu dies through Gilgamesh's arrogant behavior, parallels the story of Achilles, whose friend Patroclus dies because Achilles will not live by the rules. The theme of the long journey and return home, which governs the structure of the *Odyssey*, also informs the second half of *Gilgamesh*, when after Enkidu's death Gilgamesh journeys to the end of the world to solve the mystery of death.

Not only does Homer borrow such general themes from earlier Mesopotamian tradition, but also specific details are traceable to the East. Odysseus is a naked unkempt man when Nausicaa discovers him hiding in the bushes beside the sea on the island of Phaeacia and, in a scene of sexual tension, leads him into town; in *Gilgamesh* a harlot seduces and tames the naked wild man Enkidu whom she meets by a waterhole, then takes him to town. The never-never land of Homer's Phaeacians has much in common with the magical land of the wise Utnapishtim in *Gilgamesh* who, like Noah, survived the Flood and now lives beyond the waters at the edge of the earth. Odysseus also crosses the waters that surround the earth to consult with the wise Teiresias. His savage appearance before Nausicaa echoes Gilgamesh's wildness when he comes on Siduri, the ale-maid at the edge of the waters. Returning from Aeolus' island, Odysseus falls asleep and loses Ithaca, just as Gilgamesh falls asleep outside the house of Utnapishtim. The Odyssean *Nekuia*, "descent to the land of the dead," has much in common with a separate poem about Gilgamesh called "Gilgamesh, Enkidu, and the Underworld," which includes the detail of a man who died by falling off a roof. As Odysseus' men perish when they kill the cattle of the sun, so does Enkidu die after he and Gilgamesh kill the Bull of Heaven. In both cases a god threatens to invert the upper and lower worlds unless the gods' will prevails.

A wide range of small details in the *Iliad* and *Odyssey* are also paralleled in Eastern sources; for example, Menelaus' fathering of a child on a concubine; the splendor of Alcinous' palace; Menelaus' transportation to a paradise at the ends of the earth; Penelope's refusal to eat; the four streams of water on Calypso's island; Calypso's special food of ambrosia and nectar; the simile of the wind and the chaff; Nausicaa compared to a date palm; the metal dogs in front of the palace of Alcinous; the disappearance of the island of the Phaeacians; the sacrifice spurned by the gods; the use of protective plants (*moly* in the *Odyssey*); Odysseus' necromancy on the shores of Ocean; the name of the Sirens; the suitors' reluctance to kill one of royal stock; Penelope's bed covered with tears; the punishment by amputation of ears and nose; the radiance surrounding a divinity; birth "from oak or stone"; the bow that only the hero can draw; the archery contest; the contemptuous hurling of a leg of beef (at Odysseus); Laertes' fainting at his reunion with Odysseus – to name but a few.

A remarkable example of narrative dependence on Eastern models is found in *Iliad* 5 (330ff.), where Diomedes has wounded Aphrodite in battle. She then flees to her family in heaven for comfort. Weeping, she falls into the lap of her mother Dionê (= "Mrs. Zeus"). Dionê comforts her with mythical examples, while Hera and Athena make sarcastic remarks. Zeus calls his daughter over to him and gently advises her to stay out of battle. She should worry, rather, about love and marriage. In *Gilgamesh*, after Gilgamesh has killed Humbaba, he washes his hair and polishes his weapons and is so handsome that Ishtar, seeing him, asks that "you grant me your fruit as a gift." Gilgamesh rudely spurns the sex-goddess and recites a long list of lovers whom she has destroyed. "When Ishtar heard this, she went in a rage to her father Anu, to her mother Antu. Her tears were flowing. 'My father, Gilgamesh has insulted me, he has numbered my insults, my insults and curses!' Anu opened his mouth, and he spoke to great Ishtar, 'You did incite the king of Uruk, therefore Gilgamesh numbered your insults, your insults and curses'" (Tablet VI). In each scene an offended daughter complains before a consoling mother and a somewhat distant and bemused father. The characters are the same: the goddess of love Aphrodite = Ishtar; the god of the sky Anu = Zeus; and his wife Antu = Dionê. Here, and only here, in all of Greek literature is Dionê Zeus' consort. Dionê is a feminine form of Zeus, just as Antu is a feminine form of Anu.

Twice as many Eastern poetic motifs are found in the *Iliad* as in the *Odyssey*. There can be no doubt that Homer inherited a tradition of storytelling that crossed linguistic and cultural lines, but just how such Eastern stories passed from East to West remains unclear. There must have been not only bilingual speakers, but also bilingual singers. In the mixed population of Euboeans and Phoenicians, or coastal Syrians, archeologically attested in Italy, Crete, and Euboea, such bilingual singers must have appeared. A scribe (not a poet) literate in West Semitic writing, familiar with the ancient West Semitic tradition of creating poetic texts through dictation, tried his hand at recording Greek epic. In making suitable changes to the West Semitic writing, he invented the technological basis for the texts of the Homeric poems and for Western civilization.

Religion in Homer

The Homeric gods are a gang of ill-tempered, often ridiculous beings whose petty jealousies are unconstrained by the seriousness of human life. They are *athanatoi*, the "deathless ones," whose members have staked out spheres of interest. Yet their immortality cheats them of the seriousness that attends human decisions and human behavior. Our acts count because we are going to die, but the gods are free to be petty forever.

The anthropomorphic and human-all-too-human behavior of the Homeric gods was already the object of Xenophanes' criticism in the sixth century BC, as we have seen (p. 9). Nor do the Homeric gods fit modern notions of what a god should be. They squabble, scheme, seduce, deceive, betray, and exercise violence against one another. In the *Iliad* they take sides in the war as much as the human combatants (although Homer is vague on why they divide as they do). They have favorites and enter into battle themselves, but without serious consequences.

But the principal setting for the gods' behavior is the banquet hall, a projection into poetry of the houses of Greek aristocrats of the Iron Age. In such banquet halls – the best evidence for which is Homer's own descriptions – there was plenty of food when food was scarce and valuable, plenty of wine and the tipsiness it brings, and the enchanting song of the *aoidos*. As the *aoidos* Demodocus in the *Odyssey* sings for the royal court of the Phaeacians, so does Apollo sing for the gods, and Homer for a society for which little material evidence remains. The banquet was the good life in heaven as on earth, but on earth it was clouded by the certainty of death. A central theme of the *Odyssey* is the perverted banquet, when the good life becomes a pretext for rapine and a setting for mass murder. Forever like brattish children, the gods dine idly on Mount Olympus, a sometimes dysfunctional extended family in a happy-go-lucky never-never land mountain-top of unending sensual pleasure:

> Olympus is the abode of the gods that stands fast forever, neither shaken by winds or wet with rain nor does snow fall upon it, but the air is spread out clear and cloudless, and over it hovers a radiant whiteness. Here the blessed gods are happy all their days. (*Od.* 6.42–6)

Every modern reader of Homer wonders, "Did the Greeks really believe in such inconsequential gods?" Let us first ask how the Homeric heroes themselves approached the gods in their own religion. Several examples show how Homeric religion did not so much depend on mutual relationships with the gods as it depended on the proper performance of traditional ritual. For example, when Odysseus comes in disguise to the hut of his faithful swineherd Eumaeus, Eumaeus kills a pig in sacrifice (*Od.* 14.420–53). "And he did not forget the immortal gods, because he was of a good mind." First he cuts hair from the piglet and throws it into the fire, "for all the gods." After butchering the animal, he cuts out thick fat pieces from all its limbs and as an offering puts them on the fire and barley on top of them. When the meat is divided, he sets aside a portion "for the nymphs and for Hermes." Finally, before eating, he burns "first offerings for the immortal gods." Homer never tells us which gods exactly are intended for most of the offerings, or why only a single portion is reserved for Hermes and the nymphs, or why these gods are appropriate on this occasion, or how exactly they are to receive the portion set aside for them.

Similarly, in the opening scene of the *Iliad*, to appease Apollo's anger and stop the plague, the Greeks give up Apollo's priest's daughter Chryseis to her father Chryses, then sacrifice and purify the army at Troy (*Il.* 1.313–17); and again they sacrifice and dance and sing the *paian* (a hymn to Apollo) at Chrysê (*Il.* 1.430–87). "And the god heard them and rejoiced," and he sent a fair wind, although we learn from Thetis that at this very time Zeus and all the other gods are dining among the blessed Ethiopians (*Il.* 1.423–4). The smoke of sacrifice is wafted "to heaven," as if it were inconsequential where Apollo really was. Religion is action and sacrifice is the form of action that religion takes among the Greek heroes, while the precise relationship of gods to the ritual remains vague or contradictory. Again, when Agamemnon returns Achilles' concubine Briseis, he swears that he has not touched her and to prove his oath sacrifices a pig (19.250–6). We are not told to which god he sacrifices; it's the act that counts.

On the one hand, then, is the religious behavior of the heroes, and no doubt Homer's contemporaries, which consists in the killing of animals to establish good relationships with the invisible powers that surround us, whoever they might be. Specific forms of sacrifice are local, but sacrifice to assuage the spirits may be universal in early human religions (the appeasing power of sacrifice remains a central dogma of Christianity).

On the other hand, Homer offers us an entirely literary vision of the family of gods who live on a mountain and conduct themselves as aristocratic humans, except they cannot die. This literary vision of the divine world is Eastern in origin. In Mesopotamia the storm god Enlil rules (like Zeus) over a family and court in which the clever water god Enki (like Poseidon and Hermes) sometimes subverts his pleasure, as the goddess of sex and war Inanna/Ishtar (like Aphrodite and Athena) exercises her wiles and power, and in one story challenges the power of her sister Ereshkigal, goddess of death (like Persephone). The Greek gods enter into battle with humans, and in the West Semitic Ugaritic Baal Epic, the goddess Anat (= Innana/Ishtar/Astarte)

> begins to smite her adversaries in the valley,
> to attack them between the two cities.
> She smites the peoples dwelling on the seashore,
> wreaks destruction on the humans dwelling to the east.
> Under her are heads like balls,
> above her are hands like locusts,
> heaps of fighters' hands are like heaps of grasshoppers.
> She attaches heads around her neck,
> ties hands at her waist.
> Up to her knees she wades in the blood of soldiers,
> to her neck in the gore of fighters.[7]

In describing the gods, Homer is therefore using traditional strategies for storytelling inherited from an older non-Greek civilization. The gods' childlike behavior, and the general lack of seriousness in Homer's stories about them, reflect their foreign origin as something separate and unrelated to real religious practice. This is not to underestimate Homer's original reshaping of such traditional narrative material to create, in the *Iliad*, the curious tension between the gods' carefree world and the heroes' world of violence and pain. With skill he introduces scenes from Olympus to comment on the mortal dilemma and, in the admixture of the two worlds, impart totality to the Homeric world.

Summary: Homer's World

The historian is trying to find a real world behind Homer's descriptions, but Homer's poems are literary creations, made up of diverse elements from different times and from different literary traditions. In the *Iliad* Homer intends to create "epic distance," a feeling in the audience that all this happened long ago in a world more noble than our own. To create epic distance, the poet consciously archaizes. All weapons are bronze (though everyday implements in the similes are iron). In this world the gods appear as men as a matter of course, and conflicts on earth are paralleled by conflicts in heaven. Men were stronger then: even two today could not lift a stone that one threw easily then. There never was a Dorian invasion, nor even Dorians (except for a couple of slips). The *Iliad* is saga, where men are grander, gods are involved, and everything a little old-fashioned, a stylized world that never existed in just this form.

The *Odyssey* for its part is folktale, with its literary conventions of fulfilled prophecy, the struggle with death, the conflict of the sexes, disguise, trickery, temporary defeat, recognition, and revenge. The *Iliad* has a taste for the surreal (for example, when the river spirit rises up and attacks Achilles), but there are no monsters or dreamlike symbols of resurrected life, which densely populate the *Odyssey*. In its representation of "reality" the *Odyssey* moves across a scale with the fairy land of the Cyclops at one end, the half-magical Phaeacians in the middle, and the dung-heaped palace of Ithaca at the other end. We can never get real "history" out of the Homeric poems, but we can learn what Greeks in the eighth century BC thought about the world and about themselves. It turns out they were a lot like us.

3

The Reader's Homer

The philologist wants to know where the texts of Homer's poems come from, and what they might have looked like in their original form. The historian wants to know what in Homer might "really have happened" and what is poetic fantasy. The reader's pleasure makes such topics important because the texts of Homer have been read and studied from the moment they came into existence in the eighth century BC, and never more so than today. Superb translations in modern European languages are easy to find and widely read in secondary and university education.

The ordinary reader has no direct consciousness of the problem of text because the reader responds directly to symbolic markings on the page according to patterns of behavior learned at an early age. The text is part of "reading" and not something you think about. Nor does the reader's pleasure derive from understanding historical elements as such, but from the swift concatenation of events, the moral depth of the tale, the beauty of expression, and the logic of the plot. In this chapter let us consider how Homer manages such elements.

Ancient and Modern Readers

A modern reader's experience of the *Iliad*, in any language, is different fundamentally from what an ancient Greek might have known. We are able to read through the whole text in a few days and to see clearly its structure and the story that Homer is telling. This can never have been true in the ancient world. The first texts of Homer were not designed for a reader's pleasure, but to aid those initiated into the mysteries of writing to recreate and memorize an aural version of the poet's actual words. Perhaps in the eighth and seventh centuries texts of the *Iliad* and

Odyssey were monstrous curiosities, of inordinate expense to reproduce and clumsy to store, rare and hard to find. That's why the later much shorter poems of the "epic cycle" were far better known in the Archaic Period than the *Iliad* and the *Odyssey*, to judge from artistic representations. It is unthinkable that in the eighth, seventh, and sixth centuries BC anyone ever sat down and "read" the *Iliad* and the *Odyssey* as we read them today.

The first time the *Iliad* and the *Odyssey* were publicly performed in the ancient world, as far as we know, was at the Panathenaea in the sixth century BC, when according to pseudo-Plato (see above, p. 14) a succession of *rhapsodes* performed portions, "one man following on another as they still do now" (they are too long to have been performed entirely). Our only evidence for earlier forms of presentation of the poems is the spate of representations of Polyphemus in the early seventh century BC, suggesting that an excerpt from the *Odyssey* was circulating widely. Ordinarily a Greek might be exposed to a small part of both poems in his education, the basis of Xenophanes' complaint in the sixth century BC, but complete copies of the poems must have been exceedingly rare.

Today, by contrast, we may read the poems silently in Greek or in English. If in Greek, the reader, no matter how experienced, will puzzle constantly over strange forms and unknown vocabulary, difficulties for which elaborate commentaries for the dutiful reader exist. Homer himself seems not always to have understood the meaning of his words and of some grammatical constructions, but passes on something that has come to him with the oral-formulaic style. Reading Homer in Greek, even for the experienced, is slow and silent.

When we read in English, our eye speeds in silence over the page, taking advantage of the line breaks and the capitalizations and the word breaks and the periods and commas to take in a poetic impression whose rules have been created for the printed page. Such an experience can be thrilling, but it bears little relationship to the experience of a member of Homer's audience, where there were intimate relations, or a *rhapsode*'s audience, where the actor's art is paramount.

Homer's Style

Everyone is struck by Homer's odd style (although translators often obscure it). It is highly repetitive: one out of every eight lines is repeated at least once. Exact repetition of messages and other instructions are a related feature and are thought to reflect the poems' origins as oral dictated text. A conspicuous example is when in *Iliad* 2 Zeus prepares a false dream to send to Agamemnon, and then the dream repeats to Agamemnon Zeus' exact instructions. Then Agamemnon tells the other kings (*Il.* 2.11–15 = 2.28–32 = 2.65–9). Similar repetitions appear in Mesopotamian literature, although they are not oral dictated texts.

Above all there are the recurrent repeating epithets that so puzzled Milman Parry:

> Then with a mighty burst of anger spoke to him *swift-footed* Achilles: "You have fooled me, you god *that works from afar*, most cruel of all gods . . ." (*Il.* 22.14–15)

We now explain such usages, and similar formulaic expressions and passages, as part of the special language of the *aoidos*, assisting the singer to compose extemporaneously as he works with semantic units larger than the modern "word." The practical advantage of the repetitive, formulaic style is that it allows the poet to compose in a steady stream, while slowing the pace of the narrative by increasing the ratio between the number of "words" spoken and the unit of semantic communication. "Swift-footed Achilles" takes longer to say but just means "Achilles" (yes, he is a great athlete, but being reminded of it does not tell me anything I didn't already know or that is specifically relevant in this context).

Slowing the narrative in this way does not prevent the pace of the story from being swift as lightning, as it is in the opening of the *Iliad*, but Homer never feels under pressure to leave anything out. He drags his story out, as if he had all the time in the world. This predilection was grist to the mill of the old Analysts, who saw deviations from a clean uncluttered ideal narrative as the result of accretion, interpolations, or later revisions. Modern readers, schooled on TV, are impatient with such narrative devices and find the battle books in the *Iliad* tedious and impossibly long. Only through sheer love of narrative in any form does the reader enjoy the series of false tales that Odysseus tells in the second half of the *Odyssey*. Whoever wrote down these poems was not putting pressure on the poet to compress his narrative!

The exaggerated leisure by which the poet can tell his story is combined with distaste for suspense, a favorite device of modern storytellers. For example, when Penelope sets out the contest of the bow, Antinous declares that no man present is the equal of Odysseus, but hoping secretly that he himself can string the bow. We do not need to wonder whether he will succeed, or what will become of the arrogant Antinous, because Homer tells us what will happen:

> So he spoke, but the heart in his breast hoped that he would string the bow and shoot an arrow through the iron. Yet truly he would be the first to taste an arrow from the hands of noble Odysseus, whom he was dishonoring as he sat in the halls urging on his comrades. (*Od.* 21.96–100)

Similarly, in a famous scene the old nurse Eurycleia discovers the telltale scar on Odysseus' thigh that reveals his identity. Homer attaches to this scene of recognition a long explanation of how he got the scar in a boar hunt, and even how his maternal grandfather gave him his name. While Eurycleia holds his leg, and Homer explains the origin of the scar, we do not wonder if she will recognize the beggar as her master, because the first thing Homer tells us is that she does:

> So she drew near and began to wash her lord. At once she recognized the scar of the wound which long ago a boar had dealt him with his white tusk . . . (*Od.* 19.392–3)

It is not the question "What happens next?" that holds the attention of the audience, but the patient reenactment of a whole world: the people who live there, what they think and say, the choices they make, their pain and joy, and the events that befall them.

Not surprisingly, so leisured a style is friendly to minute descriptions of objects and events. For example, when in *Iliad* 24 Priam prepares to visit the Greek camp, servants prepare his wagon:

> Down from its peg they took the mule-yoke, a boxwood yoke with a knob on it, well-fitted with guide rings, and they brought out the yoke-band nine cubits long and the yoke too. The yoke they set with care on the polished pole at the upturned end and they cast the ring upon the thole pin and bound it fast to the knob with three turns to left and right, and after that made it fast to the post and bent the hook under. (*Il.* 24.268–74)

In the battle books of the *Iliad* appear many detailed descriptions of gory death:

For the son of Telamon, darting upon him through the throng, hit him from close at hand through the helmet with cheek-pieces of bronze and the helmet with horse-hair crest split under the spear-point, struck by the great spear and the strong hand, and the brain spurted out of the wound along the socket of the spear all mixed up with blood. (*Il.* 17.293–8)

Homer's audience has a taste for gore that a precise description satisfies, but a distaste for reference to bodily functions or explicit descriptions of sexual behavior, unfitting to the heroic world and its admiration for manly quality.

Taken to extremes, Homer's desire to say everything encourages the list, of which there are many in both poems. A common form of list is the genealogy, where a hero lists his ancestors to prove his own worthiness. In battle scenes a list of victims can intensify and magnify the action, as in *Iliad* 11 when a cornered Odysseus feels his mettle:

But first he hit peerless Deiopites from above in the shoulder, leaping upon him with his sharp spear, and then he killed Thoon and Eunomus, and then Chersidamas as he leaped down from his car he stabbed with his spear in the navel beneath his bossed shield. He fell in the dust and clutched the ground with his palm. These he left alone and struck Charops son of Hippasus with a thrust of his spear, brother of wealthy Socus. (*Il.* 11.420–7)

Where are these names coming from? Homer appears to take them from a general storehouse of names (we never hear of any of these people before or after), part of the *aoidos'* repertoire. In the greatest list in the two poems, the celebrated Catalogue of Ships in *Iliad* 2, Homer organizes real geographical information according to a complex pattern. The list has important Near Eastern parallels. For example, in the Mesopotamian creation epic *Enuma elish*, nearly one quarter of the poem that tells of the triumph of the world-builder Marduk over the forces of chaos is given to a list of Marduk's names. No doubt in oral society the list was a way of organizing information, taken over by literate Near Eastern scribes in the same way they took over other stylistic features of oral song.

Similes

A striking feature of Homer's leisured style deserving special attention is the simile. Far more common in the *Iliad* than in the *Odyssey*, the simile is a way of stopping the action, of withdrawing from it and commenting on it, enriching it, and sometimes judging it. As in Homer's description of the shield of Achilles, itself a kind of extended simile, Homer shows us an everyday world inhabited by common people in common enterprise: shepherds who protect flocks, milk cows, and harvest wheat, or humble women who weave:

> Then speedily the son of Oileus [= lesser Ajax] forged to the front, and close after him ran good Odysseus. As close as is the shuttle to the breast of a fair-girdled woman, when she deftly draws it in her hands, pulling the spool past the warp, and she holds the rod near her breast, even so close behind ran Odysseus. (*Il.* 23.758–63)

Ordinarily, the simile makes contact at only a single point with the situation it describes. In this case, in a foot race Odysseus' closeness to Ajax = the shuttle's closeness to a woman's chest. Otherwise the scenes are deliberately utterly dissimilar. On the one hand, heroic behavior on the windy plain; on the other, the protected calm and peaceful realm of creative female activity.

Many similes appeal to the natural world and especially to the predations of great cats, which in their dangerous aggression are easy to compare with warriors. Still, the point of contact will be simple. Achilles attacks Aeneas like a ravening lion:

> And on the other side the son of Peleus rushed against him like a lion, a ravening lion that men are eager to kill, a whole people gathered together, and at first the lion ignores them and goes his way, but when one of the youths swift in battle hits him with a spear, then he gathers himself with open mouth and foam swirls around his teeth, and in his heart his courageous spirit groans and with his tail he lashes his ribs and his flanks on this side and on that and rouses himself to fight and with glaring eyes rushes straight on in his fury, either to kill some man or himself be killed in the foremost throng. Even so was Achilles driven by his fury and his spirit to go up against great-hearted Aeneas. (*Il.* 20.164–75)

A driving "fury" brings together Achilles' situation and that of the lion: Achilles has not been wounded (the lion has) and Achilles has not been at first indifferent, then angry toward the enemy.

Sometimes, however, the situation in the simile can parallel that which it describes. When Odysseus sees the maidservants going off to sleep with the suitors, his heart growls and he thinks of killing them right then:

And as a bitch stands over her tender whelps growling when she sees a man she does not know, and is eager to fight, so his heart growled within him in his anger at their evil deeds. (*Od.* 20.14–16)

The point of contact is "growling," but their situations are roughly parallel. The bitch growls because her loved ones are threatened; Odysseus growls because his possessions, the maids, are taken by strangers.

In general, readers have seen in the similes the most personal touch of the poet Homer himself, as we think of poets in modern times, because in them his use of language and image is so sensual and extraordinary that we feel close there to a poet's personality. Whereas he inherited the simile as a historical device of style, common but undeveloped in Meso-potamian literature, Homer the man may well have developed it into a means for astonishing stretches, as in the following simile from a dueling scene in which Homer compares the two armies pulling at a corpse from either side to villagers tanning a bull's hide:

And as when a man gives to his people the hide of a great bull for stretching, all drenched in fat, and when they have taken it they stand in a circle and stretch it, and right away its moisture goes out of it and the fat enters in under the tugging of many hands, and all the hide is stretched to the utmost, even so they on this side and they on that were hauling the corpse back and forth in a small space and their hearts were full of hope, the Trojans that they might drag the corpse to Ilios, but the Achaeans to the hollow ships. (*Il.* 17.389–97)

Even more rarefied:

The Danaans poured in among the hollow ships, and a ceaseless din arose. And as when from the high crest of a great mountain Zeus who gathers the lightnings moves a dense cloud away, and clear to view appear all the mountain peaks and high headlands and meadows and from heaven breaks open the infinite air, even so the Danaans when they had pushed back from the ships consuming fire had rest for a little time, although there was no ceasing from war. (*Il.* 16.295–302)

What is the point of contact? Evidently the brevity of the Danaans' respite from war. Homer does not say that the dark cloud will soon return to cover the mountain, but we must presume it. First the mountain is dark, then sunlit, then dark again. Even so the Danaans are immersed in war, get a breather, then are immersed again. Homer's sophisticated audience appreciates original imagery and refined thought.

Homer and Plot

Formulas and formulaic phrases, repetition, detailed descriptions, hostility to suspense, and elaborate similes exist to support the story Homer is telling, the underlying structure of plot, the bones behind the flesh of narrative style. We take plot for granted in modern entertainment, in novels and feature films, but there is little evidence for it in pre-Hellenic literatures. A critical exception is *Gilgamesh*, which does have rudimentary plot, at least in the version preserved on the 12 tablets from Nineveh. Our sense of plot goes back directly to Homer, but in this matter as in many others he built on earlier achievements.

Narrative literature can seem like life, but in life there is no plot; verisimilitude in literature is an illusion. What is plot, that drives Homer's poems? Aristotle was the first to analyze elements of plot, which he calls *muthos* (our "myth"). He is thinking mostly about Greek tragedy, where principles laid down by Homer were refined into the modern plot so familiar today:

> . . . the proper arrangement of the incidents . . . is the first and most important thing in tragedy. We have laid it down that tragedy is a representation of an action [*mimesis praxeos*] that is whole and complete and of a certain magnitude, because a thing may be a whole and yet have no magnitude. A whole is what has a beginning and middle and end. A beginning is that which is not a necessary consequence of anything else but after which something else exists or happens as a natural result. An end on the contrary is that which is inevitably or, as a rule, the natural result of something else but from which nothing else follows; a middle follows something else and something follows from it. Well constructed plots [*muthoi*] must not therefore begin and end at random, but embody the formulas we have stated. (Aristotle, *Poetics* 1450b; trans. W. H. Fyfe, modified)

A plot, then, has three elements: a beginning, a middle, and an end. These elements are not interchangeable but have individual characteristics. Such elements, Aristotle saw, first appeared in Homer's poetry:

> In writing an *Odyssey* he did not put in all that ever happened to Odysseus, his being wounded on Parnassus,[8] for instance, or his feigned madness when the host was gathered (these being events that did not necessarily or probably lead one to the other), but he constructed his *Odyssey* around a single action [*praxis*] in our sense of the phrase. And the *Iliad* is the

same. As then in the other arts of *mimesis* a single *mimesis* means a *mimesis* of a single object, so too the plot, being a representation of an action [*mimesis praxeos*], must represent a single piece of action and the whole of it, and the component incidents must be so arranged that if one of them were transposed or removed, the unity of the whole is dislocated and destroyed. For if the presence or absence of a thing makes no visible difference, then it is not an integral part of the whole. (Ibid: 1451a)

Aristotle's words are some of the most studied in literary criticism. He seems to mean that, first, literature is not life but a "representation" (*mimesis*) – verisimilitude is an illusion. A representation of what? Of a single "action" (*praxis*) and the whole of it (which has three parts). The action of the *Odyssey* is the homecoming of Odysseus. The action of the *Iliad* is not "the war at Troy," which would not be a single object, but the anger of Achilles. In the two poems we learn all about these actions, from beginning to end, in three parts that are not interchangeable with one another.

Such remain the elements of plot in modern storytelling, whose most important form by far is the feature film. Plots in feature films are rigorously formulaic, divided into three parts separated by a "plot point," an incident that changes the direction of the story. In a 120-minute film, primary plot points appear at minutes 30 and 90 and a subordinate plot point at minute 60, the midpoint of the film.

The *Iliad* and the *Odyssey* are each eight or nine times longer than a feature film, but fall into the same tripartite structure. In the first part of the *Iliad* Achilles quarrels with his commander, who takes from him his concubine. That is plot point one, turning the action to the very long middle section (Books 2–16), where the fighting goes against the Greeks. This middle section is broken into halves at the midpoint by the embassy to Achilles in Book 9, a secondary plot point. The death of Patroclus in Book 16 is the second primary plot point, turning the story to its third section in which Patroclus is avenged and, at last, Achilles abandons his anger.

Like the *Iliad*, the *Odyssey* has a tripartite structure. The beginning is devoted to Telemachus: chaos at home and a son trying to find his father. In plot point one Odysseus escapes from the island of Calypso and the story changes as we explore Odysseus' efforts to return to his home. The revelation of his identity on Phaeacia is the midpoint of the plot, when Odysseus describes his journey home, a newborn on the verge of entering his ancient home. The final section begins when Odysseus is delivered asleep on Ithaca. Now the son will meet the

father, plot point two, and they will together resolve the conflict between those who behave against justice, taking what is not theirs, and
those who defend their homes and wives against outrage.

Summary: The Achievement of Homer

Ordinarily when we study a work of literature we have some information
about where it was composed, when it was conceived, and how it was
promulgated. In Homer's case we have none of these. Truly, Homer is
a profound mystery. He stands at the beginning of Western alphabetic
literacy, but how and why? His poems are far too long to have been
ordinary or usual. After two and a half thousand years of intense examin-
ation we cannot say what these poems were for.

The greatest obstacles to understanding have come from every generation's expectation that Homer behaved as we behave, and as those
around us behave. He sat at his desk and he wrote two long and complex poems. But overwhelming evidence reveals that he did not do this.
He came from a world about which we can only speculate, that lies at
the edge of Greek alphabetic literacy.

According to a plausible explanation, Homer dictated his poems to
someone, somewhere, sometime, perhaps on the island of Euboea in the
early eighth century BC. Certainly he was heir to a very old tradition of
oral song-making with roots in Mesopotamia. For hundreds of years
such songs had been taken down, after a fashion, in the West Semitic or
Phoenician script; now Homer was taken down in the brand new Greek
alphabet, the first technology capable of preserving a rough outline of
the phonetic qualities of human speech. The poems, or portions of
them, were thereafter the basis of Greek education, as they clearly were
in the Archaic and Classical Periods. Even today Homer is central to
humanistic education.

Once we place the man Homer in time we can take him as a witness
for how Greeks lived at that time, but to do so we must first strip away
the literary artifice by which he has made his stories interesting: plot,
character, beautiful expression, myth, fantasy, emotional and moral conflict, and the resolution of conflict. If Homer lacked such literary artifice,
he would of course cease to be so interesting; or we might say he would
not exist at all, because Homer's greatness as an *aoidos* must lie behind
someone's taking the trouble to fashion text from song in the first place.
Those who suppose that separate authors stand behind the *Iliad* and the

Odyssey imagine, apart from internal evidence, that the creation of such texts could have happened at any time, that "two Homers" could have existed in the same time and place.

Whereas philological, historical, and literary overviews of Homer's poems are of immense interest, we must now examine more closely the elements of literary artifice to see how these poems mean what they mean, proceeding from scene to scene and sequence to sequence. Let us follow the poet's exposition, remarking as we go on issues that have attracted the attention of literary historians. Herein, if anywhere, we will find Homer's lasting achievement.

Part II

The Poems

_____

4

The *Iliad*

The *Iliad* is so vast as to defy ready comprehension. Remembering that the division of the books into 24 parts according to the letters of the Greek alphabet came long after Homer dictated his text, we can none-theless see that Homer works in broad, sometimes discrete, units in building his plot. These units, or scenes, were clear enough to whoever divided the poems into 24 books each, because often a unit will corre-spond with the length of a book. The Greeks had names for these units (for example, "Helen on the Wall," the "Battle at the Ships," and the "Battle of the Gods"). Some of these units no doubt had an independ-ent status in the oral tradition, or were conjoined with other units in different ways at the hands of different singers at different times. In the days of Homeric Analysis these units were thought to have formed separate poems that editors joined to make our text, but no one believes that any more.

In reality, of course, Homer is a whole and the units of narrative I identify below are to help our analysis of this sometimes-unwieldy poem. I will use titles for these units, often of my own devising.

Invocation: "The Anger of Achilles" (1.1–7)

We associate with the genre "epic" the *Iliad*'s great length of around 16,000 lines. The danger in epic is that we lose the thread of the plot, but the prologue places the story squarely before us. The poem's first word in Greek is "anger" (*mênis*): here is a story about anger and what anger does to you, as will be clear in learning the fate of Achilles son of Peleus. "Sing, O goddess, the anger of Achilles son of Peleus." The "goddess" is that mysterious being who embodies the power of the *aoidos* to spin out a song *ex tempore*. She will help him tell how the anger came to be and all the harm it caused.

And when did this anger begin?

> From the time when first parted in strife Atreus' son, king of men, and brilliant Achilles. (*Il.* 1.5)

Homer does not launch his story *in medias res* ("into the middle of things") as often claimed, but begins at the beginning, the quarrel between Achilles and Agamemnon. The story of Achilles' anger takes place, from beginning to end, during a few days apparently in the tenth year of the war (*Il.* 2.134). Just what exactly caused this quarrel?

"Ransom of Chryseis" (1.8–611)

It was the god Apollo who brought the crisis to a head. The priest Chryses had come to the Greek camp to reclaim his daughter Chryseis, captured in a raid, but Chryseis is now the property, the "prize" (= Greek *geras*), of the chief war leader Agamemnon. One's *geras* is an outward and visible proof of one's *timê* (pronounced "*tee*-may"), a word usually translated as "honor," but which means "worth" or "value."

Agamemnon orders Chryses to leave the camp immediately. He does so, but prays to Apollo, the god he serves, for whom he has roofed a shrine. Chryses' special influence prevails and now the god serves him. Apollo fires deadly arrows first at animals, then at men, an image of plague.

Achilles, a war leader from Thessaly and king or "Big Man" (= Greek *basileus*) in his own right, calls an assembly to discuss the common peril. The reluctant prophet Calchas reveals that the fault belongs to their own commander. Agamemnon's refusal to give up Chryseis has caused the plague.

Helpless to oppose the common good, Agamemnon agrees to relinquish the girl, but only on condition that he be given someone else's *geras* so that he, the greatest king of all, might not be without honor or *timê*. If necessary, he will even take Briseis, Achilles' prize in the fair allotment. Agamemnon's bluster, and his explicit threat to Achilles' own *timê*, provokes a blunt reply, in which Achilles clearly defines the terms of their disagreement:

Glaring from beneath his brows spoke to him swift-footed Achilles, "Ah me, clothed in shame, thinking of profit, how shall any man of the Achaeans obey your words with an eager heart, to go on a journey or to fight against men with violence? It was not on account of the Trojan spearmen that I came here to fight, for they have done no wrong to me. Never have they driven off my cattle or horses, nor ever in deep-soiled Phthia, nurse of men, did they lay waste the harvest. Many things lie between us – shadowy mountains and sounding sea. But you, shameless, we followed so that you, dog-face, might rejoice, seeking to win *timê* for Menelaus and yourself from the Trojans. You pay no attention to this. And now you threaten to take my *geras* from me, for which I labored so hard, which the sons of the Achaeans gave to me. Never have I *geras* like yours, when the Achaeans sack a well-peopled citadel of the Trojans. My hands undertake the brunt of furious battle, but if ever an apportionment comes, your *geras* is far more, while small but precious is the reward I take to my ships, after I have worn myself out in the fighting. Now I will go back to Phthia. It is far better to return home with my beaked ships, nor do I intend while I am here dishonored to pile up riches and wealth for you. (*Il.* 1.148–71)

Achilles directly threatens Agamemnon's power, a frontal assault, and anger grips Agamemnon. He will in fact take Achilles' girl, Briseis. The enraged Achilles draws his sword to kill Agamemnon, which his devotion to the winning of *timê* might justify. The situation is out of control: if Achilles kills Agamemnon, the expedition will break up and the war will be lost (and there will be no story). But Athena, visible to Achilles alone, pulls him by the hair and stops his hand: if he now relents, he will later be honored ever more and receive three times as many prizes, she says.

Achilles does relent. Agamemnon may take Briseis, but at the price of an ocean of anger that now consumes Achilles' whole being. He has been publicly dishonored. He will no longer fight for scum like Agamemnon and his tawdry cause. King Agamemnon, and all who allowed him to behave in this way, will soon regret that Achilles is no longer afoot on the plain of battle. Nestor, whose great age gives him wisdom and authority, attempts to calm the captains, but matters have gone too far and they part in anger.

That is how the story begins. Such an abundance of action takes place in less than 300 lines, one of the great action sequences in literature. Homer, the inventor of plot, defines the story of the double bind: no matter in what direction a character turns, he is ruined, a characteristically Greek perception. We sympathize with Achilles, and believe that

Agamemnon treats him unfairly, but what choice does Agamemnon have? Agamemnon must replace his *geras*, which the plague forces him to relinquish, or he will be without *timê*, hardly befitting the leader of an international expedition in a world where all behavior is directed to winning *timê*. For *timê* engenders "fame" = Greek *kleos*, really "that which is heard," from *kluo* "to hear." You have *kleos* when an *aoidos* sings of your deeds, and through *kleos* you remain alive (as still today we speak of Achilles). In this way the great warrior defies the human curse of mortality. When Hector issues a challenge to the Achaeans for someone to meet him in manly duel, he says:

> But if I kill him, and Apollo gives me cause for boasting, I will take his armor and carry it to sacred Ilios and hang it on the temple of Apollo, the god that strikes from afar, but his corpse I will give back to the well-benched ships, that the long-haired Achaeans may give him burial and heap up for him a *sêma* [= "sign," that is, a mound] by the wide Hellespont. And some one will some day say, of men that are yet to be, as he sails in his many-benched ship over the wine-dark sea, "This is the *sêma* of a man that died in olden times, whom once in the midst of his greatness [*aristeia*] glorious Hector killed." So shall some man say, and my *kleos* shall never die. (*Il.* 7.87–91)

To give up his girl (= *geras*) is for Agamemnon the same as giving up the purpose for living.

Nestor attempts to stop this perilous quarrel by reminding the captains of their common goal, to take Troy, whose rulers will enjoy such dissension. But no common goal can override the personal conflict. There are no states in Homer's world, a central power to overcome the individual's desire to impose his own will on the world. The campaign against Troy is in danger of coming apart.

The Achaeans (also called Danaans or Argives) return Chryseis to her father and heralds take Briseis from Achilles' hut. Achilles goes to sit alone by the sea. He weeps and calls to his divine mother Thetis, a nymph of the sea:

> Mother, since you bore me, though to so brief a span of life, surely ought the Olympian to have delivered *timê* into my hands, Zeus who thunders on high, but now he has given me no *timê*. Truly the son of Atreus, wide-ruling Agamemnon has taken away my *timê*, for he has taken and keeps my *geras* through his own arrogant act. (*Il.* 1.352–6)

Thetis comes from the sea to comfort him. Achilles asks her to intercede with Zeus, whose will is always fulfilled: may the Achaeans, his former companions, fall to Trojan ferocity. As for his part, he will fight no more.

Homer finishes the unit with Thetis' successful appeal to Zeus, Hera's bitchy complaint about other women's influence, and the lame peace-maker Hephaestus, more successful than Nestor, brings the Olympians to their cups and their senses.

"False Dream" (2.1–210)

"The Ransom of Chryseis" explains the origin of the quarrel between Achilles and Agamemnon, and Achilles' angry refusal to fight is plot point one. The direction of the action now changes completely. The sequence of scenes that follows Achilles' withdrawal must show just how Zeus brought defeat to the Achaeans, according to Achilles' request to Thetis and Thetis' request to Zeus. Only the death of his friends can satisfy Achilles' anger. Although Homer never forgets his purpose, he now takes the opportunity to tell the "story of the Trojan War," and Achilles' presence is barely felt. In a modern film or novel it would be impossible to drop out the main character for a third of the story, as Achilles drops out here. However, the sequence of scenes, tied together by a sometimes invisible narrative thread, does give the sense that time is passing and that things are happening out there while Achilles mopes in his tent.

In order to fulfill his purpose to punish the Achaeans, according to Thetis' request, Zeus decides to send False Dream to Agamemnon. On the very next day he can sack Troy, False Dream will whisper. Zeus' purpose is evidently to lure the Achaeans onto the plain in expectation of victory where they are exposed to Trojan fury, as if they needed to be tricked into fighting.

Homer presents the ploy as burlesque. The bungler Agamemnon, after receiving the dream, concocts the cockeyed plan to invert the dream's message and tell the troops they will never take Troy. Surely the sugges-tion will only inspire them to fight harder, he is thinking, but instead the Achaean warriors run with a shout pell-mell to the boats, eager to sail home. It's a stampede for peace. Only the resourceful Odysseus can stop them.

The sequence is a joke and meant to spark laughter. Humor, something that makes you laugh or smile, resides in the perception of incongruity, and there is much humor in the *Iliad* (but almost none in the *Odyssey*). Supposedly the bronze-clad Achaeans long for nothing more in life than the *timê* that prowess in battle may bring. Yet in an instant, and on a misunderstanding, they turn tail and run! Homer's audience is peeping through: the joke appeals to fighting men who have felt the urge just to run away. The soldier–poet Archilochus, who may have lived in the seventh century BC, was to write a famous poem in which he brags how he threw away his shield and ran, for he could always get another, and other poets made the same boast. Real warriors know too much of war to believe its pieties, and what we might call antiwar themes were always part of the Greek warrior culture.

Odysseus snatches the scepter, symbol of authority, from the bewildered Agamemnon and restores order. All respectfully sit down except for Thersites, the "ugliest man who went to Troy," misshapen in body and with a pin head, an object of laughter. He is the opposite to Achilles, said to be the "most handsome man at Troy." Later tradition reported how Achilles killed Thersites because he mocked Achilles for loving the Amazon queen Penthesilea. Many commentators have taken Thersites to be the only named member of the "people" (= Greek *dêmos*), the rank and file in the poem, because of his rudeness and ugliness. Thersites complains about the war and Agamemnon's behavior to Achilles until Odysseus whacks him with the scepter, and everyone has a good laugh at his expense.

Odysseus takes the occasion to clarify the political premises by which they live: not everyone can be a king! Odysseus reminds the army, and Homer's audience, of their purpose in this war and the sureness of eventual victory. The fighting is set to begin.

"Catalogue of Ships" (2.441–887)

To magnify the battle's greatness, and in accord with his purpose to drop back and tell the "story of the Trojan War," Homer lists the combatants in the "Catalogue of Ships," which begins with the most celebrated series of similes in Homer. At first he compares the troops with birds and flies:

> And as the many tribes of winged fowl, wild geese or cranes or long-necked swans on the Asian meadow by the streams of Caystrius, fly this way and that, glorying in their strength of wing, and with loud cries settle

ever onwards, and the meadow resounds, even so their many tribes poured forth from ships and huts into the plain of Scamander, and the earth echoed wondrously beneath the tread of men and horses. So they took their stand in the flowery meadow of Scamander, numberless as are the leaves and the flowers in their season. Even as the many tribes of swarming flies that buzz to and fro in the herdsman's farm in the season of spring, when the milk drenches the pails, even in such numbers stood the long-haired Achaeans on the plain in face of the men of Troy, eager to rip them apart. (*Il.* 2.459–73)

Stacking on still more similes that emphasize the greatness of the expedition, he appeals to the Muses, who must be the same as the "goddess" of the poem's first line, to help him remember the leaders of the various contingents and the numbers of the ships in their order.

The Catalogue of Ships is famously dull reading and sometimes omitted from translations, but it is a document of great importance, the first geography of the Western world. Information in it does not always agree with information in the rest of the poem, as if the Catalogue had a life of its own. Here is a typical entry, that of the Euboeans, who lived in the long island along the eastern coast of mainland Greece, where the Greek alphabet was first used and where Homer's texts may have come into being:

And the Abantes, breathing fury, who held Euboea and Chalcis and Eretria and Histiaea, rich in vines, and Cerinthus, near the sea, and the steep citadel of Dios, and who held Carystus and lived in Styra – all these again had as leader Elephenor, follower of Ares, who was son of Chalcodon and captain of the great-hearted Abantes. And with him followed the swift Abantes, with hair long at the back, spearmen eager with outstretched ashen spears to tear the corselets on the breasts of the enemy. And with him there followed forty black ships. (*Il.* 2.536–45)

It's not clear why the Euboeans should be called the Abantes. Chalcis and Eretria were the earliest rival states in historical Greece to attract allies from abroad, according to Thucydides (1.15), and Carystus was on the extreme southern coast, but no one knows where Histiaea is or Cerinthus or Dios. The mixture of known and unknown places is typical of the Catalogue, as is the appearance of famous heroes side by side with such complete unknowns as Elephenor and Chalcodon.

The Catalogue of Ships must have been a traditional song in Boeotia, the mainland where Homer's near-contemporary Hesiod lived just opposite Euboea. For that reason, to the puzzlement of commentators, instead of beginning with the Argives Homer starts his description from the Boeotians, then spirals counter-clockwise southwest of Boeotia to the contingent from Phocis, east to Locris, further east to Euboea, then south across the island of Salamis to Argos and Mycenae. We are certainly surprised to learn that Diomedes rules Argos, whereas Mycenae just miles away is home to the great Agamemnon, probably an attempt to explain that in Homer's day Dorians rule the Peloponnesus (Diomedes is from northwest Greece, from where the Dorians came). The Catalogue drops further south to Sparta, then spirals clockwise to coastal Pylos, inland Arcadia, coastal Elis, the Ionian Islands (including Ithaca), and across the mainland to Aetolia. From Aetolia the Catalogue drops south to Crete and now in a counter-clockwise spiral picks up Rhodes, Cos, other islands near the Asia Minor coast, then heads straight back to the mainland for the Thessalian kingdoms north of Boeotia, including Achilles' Phthia and Hellas (whose name later designated all of Greece), north to Iolcus, then further west across the Pindus range to remote northwest Greece, including Dodona.

We have no evidence for the existence of maps in the eighth century BC, but Homer's organization of geography is spatial. Travelers must have had some way of organizing information about places to visit, sailors especially, and perhaps Homer's string of places moving as a spiral, first counter-clockwise, then clockwise, reflects popular lore. The Boeotian focus of the Catalogue accords with suggestions that Homer's audience may have included these very Abantes across the narrow strait that separates Boeotia from Euboea. The Catalogue is a very long list; its audience delighted in the music of the names and their associations. The much shorter Trojan Catalogue, which follows, is also a geography, organized now from north to south, from Troy to Caria, then following the southern coast of Asia Minor to Lycia, the lands of Greek settlement in the early Iron Age after around 1000 BC. The sheer mass of names in both Catalogues gives us a feeling for the immensity of the war that is about to unfold.

"Helen on the Wall" (3.121–244) and "Duel between Menelaus and Paris" (3.1–120; 245–461)

Achilles is at war with Agamemnon but the Achaeans are at war with Troy, led by the peerless Hector, son of King Priam. Before the Achaean horde (ten men for every one of the Trojans) clashes with the Trojans, before the action begins, we now meet the great Hector when he stands before all and proposes a duel between the principals, Paris and Menelaus. Any such duel of course belongs logically to the beginning of the war, not to its tenth year. Homer must have had much of this material in his repertory, reused now as a delaying action to create the illusion that a lot happens while Achilles waits for the fulfillment of Zeus' will. Homer is not concerned with the plausibility of the duel, but with the need to delay the action; he ignores realism to fulfill dramatic need.

The proposal of the duel leads effortlessly into "Helen on the Wall." We've heard about Helen already. In his abuse of Agamemnon, who threatened to take his woman, Achilles reminded Agamemnon that they came to Troy for a woman's sake. Character (originally meaning "imprint," as on a coin) supports plot, but Homer never describes character to us, as in a modern novel where we learn of a protagonist's inmost thoughts. Instead, he shows people doing things and saying things. Helen hears rumors of the duel and leaves her bedchamber to join the Trojan elders on the wall who are looking down over the plain as they might have done in the first days of the war. Already in "False Dream" we saw the intent to amuse by making fun of heroic ideals (it is incongruous for heroes to prefer home to war) and by making fun of the misshapen troublemaker Thersites. "Helen on the Wall" amuses by showing us a flighty woman's power over old men, yet turns serious in a picture of Helen's inner conflict and sorrow at her shame.

When Priam and the elders see Helen, they chatter about how beautiful she is, yet not worth the price of war. Priam calls her to his side and standing nearby assures Helen that what has happened was beyond anyone's control. Appropriate to the first days of the war, he asks who are the heroes down below on the plain, preparing for the duel. With deep irony she points out her brother-in-law Agamemnon, Odysseus (a suitor), Ajax son of Telamon,[9] and Idomeneus of Crete. When she does not see her brothers Castor and Polydeuces, she fears they have not come from shame at her behavior, "bitch that I am." In fact they are dead, but Helen's adultery has separated her from her family and all that was hers. Full of self-doubt and sorrow, but a woman who gets her way through allure – so Homer deftly shows Helen's character in this short scene.

The duel is ludicrous slapstick between a husband and his wife's lover. Homer's Paris is an effeminate lover-boy and no match for the burly Menelaus, who throws him to the ground and drags him off by his helmet. The chin strap cuts into Paris' throat. The next thing Menelaus knows, Paris has disappeared, kapoof! Where can he be? He looks around, a perfect fool.

Aphrodite has come from heaven to sweep her favorite away, carrying him to Helen's boudoir. The goddess is that irresistible destructive force called "sexual desire," who lured Helen to Paris' bed in the first place and who can do things like this. No one can resist Aphrodite, not even Zeus (as we learn later in the story). Yet darkness and death follow in the train of untamed sexual desire, even the destruction of whole cities and the ruin of whole peoples. In the bedchamber Aphrodite reminds a complaining Helen of her need for Aphrodite's protection: she must go to bed with Paris at once. Paris seems little surprised at his salvation or his good luck, or his desire to sleep with Helen at that very moment, which he does while her enraged and ridiculous husband stomps up and down the plain looking for him.

"Treachery of Pandarus" (4.1–219), "Marshaling of the Host" (4.220–363), and "Glory of Diomedes" (4.364–5.909)

When Homer comes to the end of a unit, as here, he often presents an "assembly in heaven scene" to get the action moving again. Scholars call such recurring scenes "type scenes," which follow certain general patterns and are part, we might say, of the language that the *aoidos* speaks, an element of expression with various set forms or orders of presentation. Other common type scenes are the "arming scene," the "sacrifice scene," and the "feasting scene."

A running gag about life in heaven is the unpleasant nagging of the goddesses, especially Hera and Athena, against Zeus and Zeus' need to remind the goddesses of their subordinate rank. They remind him of his place, too, and in this case of the fact that Menelaus won the duel. Because Helen was nonetheless not going back to the Achaeans, the fighting should begin again, they think.

Athena comes disguised into the ranks and encourages the Trojan Pandarus to break the sacred truce with a sneaky bowshot. The scarcely wounded Menelaus is taken off for medical attention while Homer delays still further the outbreak of general war by a second catalogue of Achaean fighting men, the "Marshaling of the Host." Agamemnon stalks down the line of troops and rallies the heroes in turn, fleshing out his admonitions with details of their lives and backgrounds. First Idomeneus, leader of the Cretans; then the "two Ajaxes" (here probably Ajax of Salamis and his half-brother Teucer); Nestor, leader of the Pylians; Menestheus, leader of the Athenians. For some reason Agamemnon singles out for rebuke Odysseus of Ithaca, who bridles, and Diomedes of Argos, which allows Homer a digression on Diomedes' father Tydeus, dead in the war against Thebes. Homer is drawing from a stock of stories about that other great war, which took place one generation earlier. Agamemnon's challenge to Diomedes' prowess sets up the first major fight sequence, which revolves around Diomedes' achievements.

Various patterns govern Homer's description of fighting. There seem to be no organized units, as there were in classical warfare, but heroes fight on their own or with occasional support from companions. Such a style of combat underlies the poem's preoccupation with *timê*, which comes to an individual fighter when he is successful, and not to a squad, corps, company, or battalion. The hero does the killing and he gets the credit. A sequence of scenes glorifying a hero is his *aristeia* ("moment of excellence").

How does one describe the violence and terror of war? How communicate the confusion, horror, and exaltation of war except through graphic description of extreme violence?

> Phyleus' son, famed for his spear, came up close and hit him with a sharp spear cast on the sinew of his head, and straight through the teeth the bronze cut away the tongue at its base. Thus he fell in the dust and bit the cold bronze with his teeth. (*Il.* 5.72–5)

No one cares if a host of nameless tin soldiers falls to the ground, so Homer often takes a moment, as each man dies, to tell us enough about him so that we feel the pathos of his death. So died the son of the Trojan Tecton ("maker"), son of Harmon ("he who fits together"); Tecton had built the ships that Paris sailed to Sparta, but in so doing he fashioned his own sorrow:

> And Meriones killed Phereclus, son of Tecton, Harmon's son, whose hands were trained to fashion all kinds of skillful work. Pallas Athena loved him above all men. It was he who built for Alexander [= Paris] the handsome ships, source of pain, made to be the curse of all the Trojans and of himself too, because he did not understand the oracles of the gods. (*Il.* 5.59–64)

The "Glory of Diomedes," which takes up most of Book 5, is the *aristeia* of one of the greatest Achaean fighters. After skirmishes between various Achaeans and Trojans, Diomedes kills a string of Trojans, then goes up against Pandarus, who had broken the truce and now wounds Diomedes as he had wounded Menelaus. The just death of the treacherous Trojan is one node in the fighting sequence. So long as Pandarus is shooting from the sidelines, Diomedes cannot kill him. But when Pandarus climbs into a chariot with Aeneas, an important Trojan ally (destined to found the Roman race, according to later tradition), Aeneas will carry him close to the fighting where he can die like a man.

There is a sort of mayhem to Homeric fighting, as in a street fight between gangs. Here Diomedes, although heavily armed in bronze and with spear and sword as weapons, nonetheless

> picked up in his hand a stone – a mighty deed – one that not two men could carry such as men are now, yet easily did he handle it by himself. With it he smashed Aeneas on the hip where the thigh turns in the hip joint – the cup, men call it – and crushed the cup-bone and broke both sinews and the jagged stone ripped the skin away. (*Il.* 5.302–10)

Aphrodite, the mother of Aeneas (and hence patron of the house of Julius Caesar, who claimed descent from Aeneas), intervenes for her son, but in a humorous scene the fearless Diomedes attacks her and wounds her hand. War is not for women, even if one is a goddess of sexual desire! Such scenes remind us that Homer's audience is not likely to have included women, at least ordinarily: in the *Odyssey*'s descriptions of *aoidoi*, the audiences are all male with the exception of Arete, a queen, on the island of Phaeacia. An all-male audience would enjoy the story of the "Wounding of Aphrodite" incorporated into the "Glory of Diomedes," telling how she fled complaining to Zeus, who gently rebuked her for inappropriate behavior. Really, Athena remarks cattily, she must have scratched herself on her brooch while encouraging an Achaean woman to have sex with a Trojan (5.421–5).

Aphrodite's entry into battle is farcical, but when Ares appears at Hector's side the Achaeans take fright. Such is Homer's grand purpose, to drive the Achaeans back, but first he wants to represent the grandeur and the complexity of war. Great wars need great opponents, and Homer establishes the prowess of the Trojan ally Sarpedon by showing him killing a certain Tlepolemus in a long duel. We need to see Sarpedon's greatness because in his finest hour Patroclus will kill him in a crucial part of the story. Ares' interference only excites Hera and Athena to oppose him, and Homer mocks the type scene of a hero's arming when he tells how Athena

> daughter of Zeus that bears the *aegis* let fall upon her father's floor her soft robe, richly embroidered, which she herself had made and her hands had fashioned, and put on the tunic of Zeus the cloud-gatherer and arrayed herself in armor for tearful war. About her shoulders she flung the tasseled *aegis*, filled with terror, all about which Rout is set as a crown and therein is Strife, Valor, and Onset that makes the blood run cold, and therein is the head of the dread monster, the Gorgon, dread and awful, a portent of Zeus that bears the *aegis*. And upon her head she set the helmet with two horns and with four bosses, made of gold and fitted with the men-at-arms of a hundred cities. Then she stepped up on the flaming car and grasped her spear, heavy and huge and strong, by which she vanquishes the ranks of men, of warriors with whom she is angry, she the daughter of the mighty sire. And Hera swiftly touched the horses with the lash. (*Il.* 5.733–48)

The description is the inspiration for thousands of ancient representations of the goddess, but in its context there is irony and humor in describing a female donning armor as if she were Achilles or Agamemnon. When she steps in the chariot of Diomedes, "Loudly did the oaken axle creak beneath its burden, for it bore a fearsome goddess and a matchless warrior" (5.838). The amusing admixture of realistic conventions – arming, traveling by chariot, fighting – with the gods' essential invulnerability comes to a climax when, with Athena's help, Diomedes stabs Ares in the guts and he screams as loud as 10,000 warriors. The poor maltreated god of war is forced to complain to his father Zeus about what a harsh lot he has in life. Zeus blames it all on his wife!

"Glaucus and Diomedes" (6.1–236)

The story is supposed to be telling us how the Trojans are defeated in accordance with Zeus' promise to Thetis, but in fact the Achaeans under Diomedes, Ajax, Odysseus, Menelaus, and Agamemnon are driving back the Trojans. Three Trojans die for every Achaean. Homer must have inherited a rich tradition telling of Achaean victories, no doubt to the descendants of such fighters of olden times, and a poor tradition telling of Trojan success. In any event, Homer takes advantage of the Achaean success to motivate Hector's brother Helenus, a seer, to send Hector into the city to supplicate Athena. Not that the action requires such supplication at this moment, but Homer wants to show us certain qualities in the man Hector, whom Achilles soon will kill.

In the meantime, the meeting of Glaucus, son of Hippolochus, from Lycia (the south central coast of modern Turkey) and Diomedes, son of Tydeus, from Argos (in the Peloponnesus), provides a respite from the gore and a quiet end to Diomedes' heroic achievements in the arena of bloody war. Diomedes has just wounded two gods and used Athena as charioteer, but he stops short when he sees Glaucus, thinking he may be a god. (Diomedes only attacked Ares on Athena's instruction.) Diomedes tells a little story about how humans suffer when they take on gods: how a king of Thrace named Lycurgus chased Dionysus into the sea, but paid a terrible price. The story is what today we call a "myth," although Homer never uses the word *muthos* in this way. This is one of the few references to the ecstatic god Dionysus, perhaps not popular among Homer's aristocratic audience.

Glaucus, too, tells a "myth" in reply, a genealogy that contains the story of Bellerophon, who slew the ferocious Chimera, an Eastern folktale that contains the only reference to writing in Homer (see above, p. 11). Folklorists call this story type "Potiphar's wife" after Joseph in the Bible, betrayed by the lustful wife of Potiphar and imprisoned. In Glaucus' story, the queen of Ephyre (Corinth) wished to sleep with handsome Bellerophon, but he rejected her. She told her husband the king that Bellerophon had made a pass at her. The king could not kill his guest, as he fully deserved, without violating the sacred customs of *xenia*, so sent him to the queen's father in Lycia bearing the folded tablet with "baneful signs."

Diomedes remembers that his grandfather had entertained Bellerophon, making the heroes *xenoi*, "guest-friends," who cannot therefore fight one another. To celebrate the renewed relationship of *xenia*, the men exchange armor. Because Glaucus' armor was made of gold (not very likely) and Diomedes' of bronze, Diomedes got much the better deal, Homer remarks. But what exactly the poet meant by this bizarre exchange no one has ever explained.

"Hector and Andromache" (6.237–529)

In the rest of Book 6 Homer shows Hector in his roles as son of Hecuba, brother to Paris, brother-in-law to Helen, husband to Andromache, and father to Astyanax ("king of the city"). Achilles may question why he should risk his life fighting on the windy plain, but Hector knows very well: to protect the life of the city and its complexities of family relationships united by respect and love. Although he and the city are doomed, yet he must behave as if his efforts can make a difference.

Hector finds his mother in the marvelous palace and refuses a glass of wine; this is not the time. Hecuba takes a finely woven cloth of Sidonian manufacture and in a procession carries it to the temple of Athena (the only time that Homer refers to a freestanding temple). The priestess places the cloth on the knees of the goddess, but the goddess denies the prayer.

Meanwhile Hector goes to Helen's bedroom, where handsome Paris has finished his lovemaking. Hector upbraids his brother for inaction. The always cheerful Paris says that he will try harder, while the seductive Helen tries to get Hector to relax, to sit down. As he refused a glass of wine from his mother, he courteously refuses her request too and hastens to his own home to visit his wife Andromache and their child Astyanax. But she like Helen has gone to the wall. He meets her at the Scaean Gate as he is about to go back onto the plain.

Hector and Andromache at the Scaean Gate is one of the most celebrated scenes in literature. Andromache begs Hector not to return to the fight and paints a picture of what will happen to their child, now asleep in a nurse's arms, if he ever loses his father. As a wife and mother it is natural for her to fear the worst and to try to prevent it from happening. Hector explains that it is not his choice to fight or not to fight. He and his family would lose *timê* if he hung back. It is his duty to fight as a son, a husband, and a member of the community.

Then he paints a gloomy picture of what will happen to Andromache, raped and enslaved and their son murdered if the city falls. Hector reaches down to the child Astyanax, who cries, frightened by the awful helmet. Hector puts the helmet on the ground and now the child recognizes him: Hector the father, not Hector the warrior. In a scene of delightful pathos Hector and Andromache laugh as loving parents.

The listener to "Hector and Andromache" knows that Hector's gloomy vision of the future will come to pass. Hector, Andromache, and Astyanax are a family, contrasted with the fruitless union of Paris and Helen, built on lust, leading nowhere except to death. Their self-indulgence, their slavery to selfish pleasure, will bring the death of the city, a collection of homes and of the families that reside therein.

"Duel between Hector and Ajax" (Book 7)

The entire span of the *Iliad* is 51 days, but almost the entire poem is devoted to four days (Books 3–22). We have not yet completed the first day of fighting when Hector returns to the plain, now in the company of Paris. We might expect the sun to set, the close to a fine day, but the scene of "Hector and Andromache" also leads us to expect immediate action. As often in the poem, the gods intervene to move the action ahead. At Apollo's instigation, Hector suddenly issues a challenge to the Achaeans to fight a duel – still one more scene, like the "Catalogue of Ships," "Helen on the Wall," and the "Duel between Menelaus and Paris," that belongs to the early years of the war.

The "Duel between Menelaus and Paris" was a circus, but the duel can allow the poet to exemplify manly and virtuous behavior. Hector declares that he will give an honorable burial to his opponent, if he should fall, and he expects the same treatment, but the victor can keep the armor. Noble men in a noble enterprise.

At first Menelaus volunteers to fight Hector, but is quickly suppressed. He's no match for him (although he has done very well on the battle-field) and anyway that morning was in a duel with Paris. Nine heroes volunteer. To decide, each marks a chit and puts it in a helmet. Here Homer might have referred to writing, if he knew about writing. A chit flies out and the herald walks it down the line until Ajax recognizes the mark.

The duel is interesting for its stylized behavior. The opponents come together, Ajax with his odd shield "like a city-wall," evidently a reminis-cence in epic of a Bronze Age shield. Each declares that he is a powerful man, a form of poetic martial verbal abuse sometimes called "flyting" (= Scots "contention"). In the Classical Period the hoplite fighter carried a single heavy thrusting spear that he never threw, but in Homer each man carries two javelins. First Hector throws, but Ajax's shield holds (in Homeric fighting the first throw is never successful). Then Ajax throws and pierces Hector's shield and corselet, but otherwise does no damage. Now each man takes his second javelin and uses it to thrust at his opponent. Hector is wounded slightly. Evidently they now discard the spears, because the next we hear they pick up huge stones and throw them at one another. As usual the first cast fails. Ajax's stone knocks down Hector, but he soon recovers. Having exhausted their javelins and thrown their rocks, they would now ordinarily draw their short swords and slash away in close quarters, but to underline the stylized, formal character of this duel, heralds at this point move in to separate them. Each man has proven worthy. From mutual respect, each gives the other a gift, equals in the game of honorable behavior. It is like a sporting event. War and the athletic contest come together closely in the "Duel between Hector and Ajax."

It seems odd that Homer has put on two duels in a single day, but the audience is swept up in the flood of the narrative and does not have a good grip on units of time. Such events do not lead to anything later in the poem, but explore the nature of the war and the personalities involved. We have learned about Ajax (the greater) and Menelaus and Odysseus and Idomeneus and about the Trojans Hector, Priam, and Paris (and Helen). To end the long exposition Nestor calls for a truce to bury the dead, and in still another striking transposition to the beginning of the war Nestor recommends that the Achaeans build an earthen wall to protect the ships: in the tenth year of the war! Simply, Homer is going to need this wall in the upcoming fighting, and so he puts it in place.

In the meantime the Trojan council meets to consider giving up Helen and the treasure that Paris stole, a conversation belonging to the first days of the war. Paris will give up the treasure, he says, but the woman, never. Treachery and injustice doom the Trojans, including the admirable Hector and his lovely family.

After the wall is built, Poseidon and Apollo on Olympus remember an earlier wall that they built for the Trojan king Laomedon, the walls of the city itself, and fear that this new wall might cloud their glory. Zeus thereby looks ahead and gives permission that they destroy this earthen wall when the war is over. As in similes, where he opens a window into the narrative and carries the listener away into surprising parallel worlds, so in passages like this Homer places the events of the war in a greater frame under the gaze of eternity, when the war at Troy, for all its glory, was gone without a trace.

"Trojans Triumphant" (Book 8)

Having presented the personalities and background of his story, Homer needs to prepare the midpoint of his plot, when Achilles refuses the embassy that would have him return to the war (Book 9). For the audience to feel a need for the embassy, we need to see the Achaeans in full retreat. It is not the overwhelming defeat that Zeus promised to

Thetis, which will come later, but a dangerous setback that will justify the embassy. In fact, the Achaeans have so far bested the Trojans in general and in most encounters. Somehow Homer has to accomplish the discomfiture of the Achaeans without killing or wounding his principal fighters, Odysseus, Agamemnon, Menelaus, and Diomedes, whose undoing is reserved for the dire fighting to come. He does this by having Zeus somewhat brusquely take control of the situation and send down thunderbolts that terrify the Achaeans and unman their will. Even so the Achaeans rally and the minor hero Teucer (half-brother of greater Ajax) has an *aristeia*, as if Homer cannot hold himself back from celebrating an Achaean hero.

In heaven, Zeus forbids the gods to interfere, especially Athena and Hera who hate Troy and have helped the Achaeans already, and he announces his power in the image of a tug of war: if all the other gods held a rope and tried to budge him, he would pull them all up, along with Earth and Sea. Zeus ascends his chariot and rides to Mount Ida behind Troy, an image repeated countless times in art after Homer. The sad mortals fight on the windy plain below, but Zeus holds up his scales to see to which side the war will incline. Down sinks the scale of the Achaeans, up rises that of the Trojans, in case any listener is unclear about where the story is going. The stunning image of Zeus as holder of the balance of fate may have its ancestry in Egyptian religion – the weighing of a dead man's heart to see if he led a just life, illustrated in the Egyptian New Kingdom Book of the Dead (second half of the second millennium BC), but here all religious meaning is lost. Zeus has willed that the Achaeans suffer and the balance reveals the certainty of his will. The thunderbolt that crashes in front of Diomedes' car, as Diomedes closes on Hector, is proof positive that he favors the Trojans, which Diomedes understands and so allows Nestor to drive him from the field.

Hector expresses exultation at the clear signs of divine preference in two speeches, one to the troops and one to his horses (8.173–97), but to draw out his story Homer has Agamemnon rouse the Achaeans again (Zeus approves with an eagle omen). The Achaean archer Teucer kills many, but after Hector smashes him with a rock, Zeus remembers his intention to favor the Trojans. Hector's assault against the ditch and the wall is so furious that Hera and Athena cannot stop themselves from arming and mounting their cars, and they desist only when Zeus threatens them with violence.

Zeus rides back from Ida to Olympus and sits upon his throne and threatens the goddesses once again. They should not complain so much:

Patroclus will die, Zeus predicts, and then Achilles will return, an outcome unfriendly to the Trojans whom the goddesses hate. By his prediction Zeus keeps the outlines of the big story clear, and Homer whets
our appetite to learn just how these events will play out. When an
overconfident Hector and the Trojan fighters camp on the plain beyond
the Achaean wall, we believe in the Achaeans' mortal danger and their
need to do something about it.

"Embassy to Achilles" (Book 9)

The "Embassy to Achilles" is to many the single best-known sequence
in the *Iliad*, a model for the study of persuasion and the midpoint of the
plot. In the "Ransom of Chryseis" we learned the cause of Achilles'
anger; here we see how Achilles' anger has changed him and the way
that he sees the world.

Much has happened since Zeus promised Thetis that he would avenge
Achilles' wrong, but Homer has been more interested in telling the
story of the Trojan War than in staging the defeat of the Achaeans. The
Achaeans were winning under the leadership of the brilliant Diomedes,
who even wounded Aphrodite and Ares in his prowess and who killed
Hector's charioteer and would have killed Hector, too, had not Zeus
intervened with a thunderbolt. Now Homer wants to bring his story
back to Achilles, whose anger has driven him to abandon and to curse
his comrades. Homer baldly declares the Achaeans to be disheartened,
as we have seen, and places the emboldened Trojans arrogantly camping
on the plain. In an astonishing simile, their campfires appear as many as
stars in the night sky when a cloud has passed.

In the Achaean camp, the defeatist Agamemnon repeats the earlier
scene in "False Dream," declaring before the troops that they can never
take Troy and should return home, but this time he means it. The
earlier scene was comical and mock-heroic when everyone ran pell-mell
to the ships; now the scene is deadly serious and no one runs. The
stalwart Diomedes chastises Agamemnon for his weakness, and Nestor
sees an opportunity to bring Achilles back into the fight.

The captains withdraw into council, and Nestor explicitly accuses
Agamemnon of having dishonored Achilles and bringing them to this
pass. "Yes," Agamemnon agrees, "*atê* [pronounced '*ah*-tay'] took hold
of me" (9.116). By *atê* ("madness") Agamemnon means a sort of personified force that takes away one's good sense, as when we say "he was

beside himself." It is not at all clear that Agamemnon accepts responsibility for what he has done, other than fallen victim to *até*, but he agrees to send many wonderful prizes, an abundance of *geras*, to restore Achilles' *timê* and palliate his anger, just as Thetis had predicted. He will give 7 tripods, 10 talents of gold, 20 cauldrons, 12 strong horses, 7 beautiful women skilled in goodly handiwork, and Briseis, with whom he has never had intercourse. Also, he will give 20 women from Troy, when they take the city, and he will even marry one of his three daughters to Achilles (so that Achilles will be his son-in-law!). Homer appears not to know the story made famous by Greek tragedy that Agamemnon killed one of his daughters to secure fair winds when the fleet set out from Aulis to Troy. Agamemnon will throw in three nice cities, too,

> if he but cease from his anger. Let him yield – Hades, I think, is not to be soothed nor overcome, and for this reason he is most hated of all the gods. And let him submit himself to me, because I am more kingly, and I am older in years. (*Il.* 9.158–61)

Three men carry the offer to Achilles' tent: Odysseus, with his persuasive speech, the greater Ajax, the mighty warrior (but why not Diomedes?), and a character who appears out of thin air, Phoenix, Achilles' tutor. Also, two heralds follow. Here we seem to observe the oral singer making adjustments to his song as he goes, but not always getting it right, because instead of saying that the three men walked along the sea (or the five men, counting the heralds), he says "the *two of them* walked along the loud-resounding sea" (*Il.* 9.182). Homeric Greek has a dual number (used of "the two Ajaxes") in addition to the singular and plural of English, and here he uses the dual form of the pronoun and the verb (that is, he doesn't actually say "the two of them"). Later he slips back into the plural number when referring to the members of the embassy. Many explanations have been offered for this anomaly, but the best explanation seems to be that Homer has inherited a version of the embassy where Phoenix was not included. Phoenix has an important role to play in Homer's embassy, but he comes from nowhere in the story. Homer brought in Phoenix, then, but did not always adjust the dual number. Here we see the *aoidos* in action; as dictated texts, the *Iliad* and the *Odyssey* were never revised to smooth out irregularities and *longueurs*.

The embassy finds Achilles playing a lyre that he took on the same raid when he captured Chryseis and Briseis. He is singing "the deeds of men," the only reference in the *Iliad* to *aoidic* poetry, though Achilles is no professional singer. The *Odyssey*, by contrast, refers to the *aoidoi* repeatedly. As a gracious host Achilles feeds the men, who then deliver their message. Odysseus begins, repeating word for word, in accordance with oral style in the reporting of messages, Agamemnon's lavish offer, but omitting Agamemnon's impossible last words about being more kingly. Odysseus appeals to Achilles' lust for recognition and *timê* that so much *geras* will confer. By returning, Achilles will also help his companions, who are suffering, and in return for such behavior they will honor him all the more. And now is his best chance to kill Hector, Odysseus adds.

Achilles' renowned reply exemplifies perfectly his state of mind, his ineradicable anger over how he has been treated. The speech *is* his anger. He hates like the gates of Hades one who says one thing, but holds another in his heart (behavior in which Odysseus in the *Odyssey* takes pride). He finds no force in their tempting him with *timê*, because, as anyone can see, merit is not necessarily rewarded. Death awaits all and therefore all are equal, the meritorious and the unmeritorious. Presumably they have come to Troy to avenge the theft of a woman, he says, but their commander, himself a coward, indulges in such theft. Why should anyone die, therefore, to restore Helen? As for Hector, let Agamemnon fight him – if he is the "best of the Achaeans" as he claims. He should not have dishonored his greatest fighter. Tomorrow Achilles will pack his things and sail home. As for Agamemnon's *geras*, they can never be enough because Achilles' life is not for sale. And his life is at stake. As for Agamemnon's daughter, let him find someone of suitable social standing, because Achilles is clearly not of sufficient rank. When life is lost, no gifts and no woman will bring it back. According to a prophecy, Achilles can gain glory but die young, or live long without glory, a course which he may well now choose, he threatens, given the emptiness of martial endeavor. He advises them all to go home, just as he will certainly do. They will need another plan to save themselves. This one isn't working. So great is the anger that consumes him.

Achilles' reply, though anger bursts at every seam, nonetheless meets the logical demands of Odysseus' entreaty: he cannot accept the offer because he has rejected the values that the offer presumes, the values according to which he had always lived until Agamemnon, his political superior but martial and moral inferior, showed him how empty such values are. Achilles dismisses the embassy and asks that Phoenix, his tutor, stay.

Probably Homer has himself invented Phoenix, who represents the sentimental obligations that a man holds to his family and the need to accede to a suppliant's appeal. Phoenix tells an interesting story about his own life: how he slept with his father's mistress, then was impotent because of his father's curse. Achilles' father Peleus received him as a suppliant and turned over the young child Achilles to him for rearing (even so should Achilles accept Agamemnon's supplication). Phoenix *is* Achilles' father, in a sense, and as a father he expects Achilles to bring him renown, to do him credit. Even the gods, Phoenix says, can be persuaded; so Achilles, who is just a man, should be persuaded too.

Phoenix tells a rather obscure allegory about divinities, "Prayers," who follow in the footsteps of a personified *Atê*, the very force that Agamemnon invoked to explain his own unwise behavior. *Atê* is swift and always outruns Prayers, Phoenix says. If you give in to Prayers (after being infected with *Atê* Phoenix means, as Achilles has been, he implies), then all goes well. But if you deny Prayers, then *Atê* pursues you all the more. In other words, things only get worse if you refuse to accept fair amends honestly given.

First, straight advice from Phoenix, then an allegory, now the complex "Myth of Meleager" about the hero from Aetolia (the southwestern corner of mainland Greece) who killed the terrible Calydonian boar. Trouble on the hunt led to war between the Calydonians and the neighboring Curetes, in the course of which Meleager killed his uncle, his mother's brother. Hating her own son for this, Meleager's mother cursed him. In resentment at the curse Meleager locked himself in his room with his wife. Although the Calydonians offered him many gifts to return to the war, only when fire reached his door did he return, by then receiving *timê* from no one. Moral: let not this be your fate, Achilles.

Odysseus appealed to Achilles' love for glory, but Phoenix appeals to his sense of moral behavior. The world is made in such and such a way. If you are harmed, you should accept recompense; then life can go on. Meleager's attitude was understandable, but because he took it too far, he got nothing in the end. That's the way the world is.

Achilles' reply is curt:

> Phoenix, old sire, my father, nurtured of Zeus, in no way do I have need of this *timê*. I receive my *timê*, I think, by the allotment of Zeus. (*Il.* 9.607–8)

Some commentators have taken Achilles' strange and radical proclamation to imply his discovery of an entirely different way of structuring values, similar to the modern Western practice where guilt, not shame, is the principal feeling when one has transgressed moral laws, the allotment of Zeus. Such an attitude toward good and bad conduct is Egyptian in origin, but was refined by Jews and Christians, so that it is familiar to us. The sanctions of guilt are internal: one's feelings of remorse; that's us. Shame, by contrast, comes from falling short of an ideal pattern of social conduct; that's the Homeric warrior. The sanctions of shame are external, as here Achilles' *geras* (prize) is tantamount to his *timê* (honor). Asian civilizations still today remain "shame cultures" in which "loss of face" leaves little reason to go on living, and in Achilles' extraordinary claim to indifference about what people think of him, his rejection of shame culture, we see Homer's moral genius.

Achilles nonetheless concedes that on the next day he and Phoenix will consider whether to depart or not – he has softened his position. Now the greater Ajax makes the shortest plea, noting that if you kill a man, one takes money and lets it go; this quarrel is over something much less important, a woman, and they have even offered him seven women more. Obviously Achilles has a heart of stone, a man who will allow his companions to die for the sake of a woman.

Ajax's appeal to camaraderie has the greatest effect on Achilles, yet his anger is too great. He yields one point: he will not fight until fire comes to the ships. Only then will he intervene.

"Song of Dolon" (Book 10)

The story about a night raid against the Trojans neatly occupies the whole of Book 10. The *Doloneia* is a splendid piece of work with an eerie cut-throat mood showing us a side of the war we have not seen: the clandestine operation across enemy lines through oceans of corpses to kill still more men and gain intelligence.

The *Doloneia* is the best candidate for a substantial interpolation into the eighth-century text that Homer dictated. No reference is made elsewhere in the *Iliad* to events in it, and some stylistic studies have suggested differences from the other books. On the other hand, the *Doloneia* refers explicitly to the situation set up before the embassy to Achilles took place: the Trojans are camped on the plain expecting victory the next day, and each side wishes to learn about the other's intentions. The poem requires a respite from the large movement bounded by the beginning of Achilles' anger in the "Ransom of Chryseis" and its outburst in the "Embassy to Achilles," and the *Doloneia* provides it. Before the fighting begins on the next morning, we must give heart to the Achaeans, so depressed that on the preceding day Agamemnon was willing to crawl on the ground before Achilles. We cannot begin with defeat the great battle that will end with Achaean defeat, when Zeus's will and Achilles' prayer to Thetis are fulfilled. The Achaeans need encouragement at this moment, and the success of the night attack provides it. Homer makes use of older material, perhaps, but he has reformed it to suit his dramatic intentions.

With the Trojan fires burning near, and Achilles unwilling to help, the Achaean captains rouse one another and decide to send Diomedes and Odysseus into the Trojan camp to discover what they can. In the arming of the spies appears one of the few certain references to a Mycenaean artifact, the boar's tusk helmet that Odysseus takes from a certain Meriones:

> And Meriones gave to Odysseus a bow and a quiver and a sword, and about his head he set a helmet made of hide, and with many tight-stretched thongs was it stiffened within, while without the white teeth of a boar of gleaming tusks were set thick on this side and that, well and cunningly, and within was affixed a lining of felt. (*Il.* 10.260–5)

The helmet was passed down for several generations until it came to Meriones, so Homer may well have seen one himself, rather than have inherited the description from hundreds of years before.

At the same time, the Trojan Dolon, an egregious fool, sets out to spy on the Achaeans. Hector has arrogantly promised to give Dolon Achilles' horses as a reward, so confident is Hector of a swift victory on the next day. Diomedes and Odysseus run Dolon down, humiliate him, extort information, then summarily cut off his head. To Homer's warrior audience Dolon is a comic figure, ridiculous in his pretensions, and his killing is no more pathetic than a cat killing a mouse.

Before dying Dolon tells his captors about the Thracian king Rhesus, newly arrived with fine horses and many men, and the relentless duo sneak into the ranks and like heroes in a video-game dispatch one after the other. As Diomedes kills, Odysseus pulls aside the dying bodies to make a pathway for the horses, who may balk at riding over human corpses! They kill Rhesus himself, steal his fine horses, and, curiously, ride them triumphantly back to camp, the only reference in the poems to riding horseback.

Events in the *Doloneia* agree with the bloodthirsty level on which much of the war is conducted. Precisely such conduct was a principal activity of the martial American Indians of the northern plains during the nineteenth century – stealing into an enemy's camp, killing some of the enemy as they slept, stealing horses, murdering captives, then riding away bareback. Such tribesmen also carried bows and arrows as principal weapons, just as Odysseus carries bow and arrows here, which he never uses. Diomedes and Odysseus in fact learn nothing about the enemy's intentions, but no one seems to care.

Critics of the *Doloneia* object to its cut-throat morality, but such criticism is unhistorical. Or they find the book irrelevant, but an exciting chase through shadows over mounds of corpses and the undoing of a careless enemy will justify itself. We are not surprised on the next morning to find the Achaeans now ready to attack.

"Wounding of the Captains" (11.1–595)

Just so, when the fighting begins the next day, Homer describes in delicious detail the extraordinary martial feats of Agamemnon, Achilles' bitter enemy, whom Achilles had called a coward and a "woman." This is our chance to see Agamemnon in action, who claims to be "best of the Achaeans." First, Agamemnon arms himself (11.15–46), Homer's most elaborate example of the arming type scene, except for the later arming of Achilles (19.369–91). When a warrior arms, he puts on or takes up the same items in the same order. Agamemnon puts on greaves, then silver ankle-pieces, then the corselet, a gift from Cyprus decorated by bands of lapis lazuli, gold, and tin and inlaid with lapis lazuli serpents. Then he takes up his sword, his shield "that sheltered a man on both sides" (11.32), decorated with circles of bronze, bosses of tin, and the head of the Gorgon. Then he takes up his helmet with two horns and horsehair crest and, at last, two spears.

So equipped, Agamemnon makes mincemeat out of the Trojans in a splendid *aristeia*. Zeus even dissuades Hector from approaching Agamemnon, so clearly in his glory, until Agamemnon should be wounded, when Zeus promises the advantage will turn. Over 200 lines later Agamemnon is still chopping away, until at last he takes a wound that pains him like the stabbing a woman feels while giving birth.

Now it is Hector's turn to kill. In the rhetoric of mayhem, Homer uses a focusing device when he delivers the lead to a new character, a rhetorical clue to the listener: "Who was the first to die?" he asks, then we get a long list.

Agamemnon has been wounded; now it's Diomedes' turn, whom Paris hits with an arrow. Diomedes complains that real men fight with spears (so much for Paris), but he *is* wounded and Odysseus moves in to cover him. Odysseus has a little *aristeia*, and many Trojans fall before he too is wounded. Now it is the turn of the greater Ajax, who kills many more Trojans, but he too is driven back.

Homer is setting up his second plot point, the death of Patroclus, which will bring Achilles back in the action and turn the story to its resolution in the death and ransoming of Hector. The wounding of the heroes Agamemnon, Diomedes, and Odysseus and the retreat of Ajax make inevitable this turn of events.

"Plan of Nestor" (11.596–848)

Paris has wounded Machaon, the army physician, and the provident Nestor carries out the wounded man in his car. Achilles sees them as he cranes his neck and watches from his compound, eager to know how the battle is going. He sends Patroclus to find out who has been wounded. Patroclus has so far kept in the background, but now he speaks for the first time and quickly becomes a center of attention.

Nestor wishes to entertain Patroclus and brings out an heirloom cup, the illustrious "Cup of Nestor." As we saw earlier (pp. 32–3), a cup from Ischia in the Bay of Naples reads "This is the cup of Nestor . . . ," implying a written text of the *Iliad* if the cup is Homer's own detail and not a traditional element in oral verse-making. Although Patroclus is anxious to return to his tent, once he sees that it is Machaon who is wounded, Nestor holds him by relating his martial exploits as a young man in the northwestern Peloponnesus. Why, he killed a man named Itymoneus in a cattle raid taken in reprisal against King Augeias of Elis (whom Heracles killed according to later tradition). He describes the war that followed. Many think that such local stories as Nestor's originated in real events, preserved by the *aoidoi*, and that somehow Homer has heard poems sung in the western Peloponnesus.

Nestor is garrulous but a deviser of plans, and he suggests that Patroclus put on Achilles' armor to make the Trojans think Achilles has returned. This will give relief to the Achaeans, who are doing very badly. From

Nestor's plan comes an unquenchable anguish for Achilles and a new object for his ocean-sized anger.

"Battle at the Wall" (Book 12)

Earlier Homer described the building of a mysterious wall to protect the ships (they had done fine for nine years without one), and now he invokes the mythical language of the universal flood to explain the wall's eventual disappearance:

> When all the bravest of the Trojans had died and many of the Argives – some killed and some were left – and Priam's city was sacked in the tenth year, and the Argives went back in their ships to their dear native land, then did Poseidon and Apollo take counsel to sweep away the wall, bringing against it the might of every river that flows forth from Ida's mountains to the sea. (*Il.* 12.13–18)

Homer's point of view is striking, a flash-forward into his own day from which he looks back on the events he is now describing. There is no doubt about how the war will end, no suspense in the mind of the audience. The destruction of the wall symbolizes the break between the heroic past and Homer's own time, but the language of the great flood, sweeping all before it, may go back to the Mesopotamian story of the Flood that drowned the world. No Greek could have had direct experience of disastrous flood, and in such passages we may glimpse the great antiquity of elements in Homer's poems.

While Patroclus makes his way back to Achilles' tent, Homer intensifies the danger to the ships and heightens the urgency of Nestor's plan to send out a substitute Achilles. Hector is actually attacking the wall, and the whole of Book 12 is given to this monumental battle. A ditch with dangerous stakes fixed in it lies before the wall, which has several gates, we now learn. Fearful of the ditch, the Trojans dismount, break into six companies, and prepare to attack as the Achaeans scurry inside.

Homer's language in this long battle sequence, which leads to Hector's temporary victory, draws from the traditional theme of the sack of a city, in some versions no doubt Troy's sack. Once (12.177–8) Homer even refers to the wall as being "stone" to which fire is applied, although the wall is neither stone nor is fire applied to it. Throughout, the imagery is of the sacking of a city, not the taking of a defensive wall:

> In their might they sought to break the great wall of the Achaeans. The towers of the fortifications they dragged down and overthrew the battlements and pried out the supporting beams that the Achaeans had set first in the earth as buttresses for the wall. These they tried to drag out and hoped to break the wall of the Achaeans. However not even now did the Danaans give ground from the path, but closed up the battlements with bulls' hides, and cast down at the enemy, as they came up against the wall. (*Il.* 12.256–64)

A fearful omen of an eagle attacking a living snake proves that the Trojan victory will be temporary, but Hector rejects the omen with a snarl: such infatuation is expected in a man doomed to die (12.195–250). After thrilling fighting, the Lycians under Sarpedon and Glaucus (who earlier exchanged his gold armor for Diomedes' bronze) attack one of the gates. Sarpedon sums up the heroic creed (12.322–8): if one could somehow escape death altogether, war would make no sense; but since no man escapes death, you might as well behave honorably.

So motivated, they attack the wall with such fury that its defender Menestheus, king of Athens, calls to the two Ajaxes, who like to fight together (they are unrelated). Greater Ajax, son of Telamon, rushes to Menestheus' aid and kills many. Then up comes Hector, who picks up an enormous stone, hurls it against the gates, breaks the bolt, and the gates swing open. The wall is breached.

"Battle at the Ships" (Book 13)

It would be too easy for Hector and the Trojans simply to enter the camp and fire the ships, all the while that Patroclus makes his way back to the tent of Achilles. Homer needs to slow down the action so that he can continue to entertain through graphic descriptions of violence. Here is a striking quality to his style: although the action is swift, there is no hurry to finish the story, as if he had all the time in the world. We wish we could explain Homer's predilection for so leisurely a pace, but can only conclude that his amanneusis admired and enjoyed it. Homer must have been the master of stringing things out: no other poet composed poems so long, as far as we know.

Here he slows the action by the "Battle at the Ships" in which Hector's drive is checked, thanks to Zeus' inattention and Poseidon's instigation. Into the drama Homer brings all the great marshals (except Achilles) from both sides, and we get our best picture yet of who are the leaders of the opposing armies. For the Achaeans (Diomedes, Agamemnon, and Odysseus are wounded) the leaders are the two Ajaxes, Teucer (the brother of Ajax son of Telamon), Antilochus (son of Nestor), Menelaus, Idomeneus king of the Cretans, and Menestheus king of Athens (not the celebrated Theseus, who was his predecessor); for the Trojans it is the four brothers Hector, Paris, Deiphobus (who after Paris' death will be Helen's consort), and Helenus (the prophet), as well as Aeneas (son of Aphrodite).

When Homer says that Zeus' attention wandered from the field of battle, the listener knows that a digression is on the way, in this case a very long one: not until two and a half books later does he return the battle to the position it was in at the end of the "Battle at the Wall."

Earlier Poseidon and Hera had threatened to oppose Zeus' plan for the Achaean defeat and now Poseidon takes advantage of Zeus' careless inattention to enter the battle in person. Poseidon comes to Troy in an influential description:

He let harness beneath his car his two bronze hoofed horses, swift of flight with flowing manes of gold, and with gold he clad himself about his body and grasped the well-made whip of gold and stepped up on his car and set out to drive over the waves. Then gamboled the sea-beasts beneath him on every side from out of the deep, for well they knew their lord and in gladness the sea parted before him. Most swiftly they sped on, and the axle of bronze was not wetted beneath and to the ships of the Achaeans did the prancing steeds bear their lord. (*Il.* 13.23–31)

Every artistic representation of Poseidon/Neptune goes back to this description, as Herodotus understood when he remarked that Homer and Hesiod "are the ones who taught the Greeks the descent of the gods, and gave the gods their names, and determined their spheres and functions, and described their outward forms" (Herodotus 2.53).

Taking the form of the prophet Calchas, Poseidon rouses the two Ajaxes and a catalogue of others. Many die as the fighting rages. Poseidon takes on a new form and encourages the Cretan king Idomeneus, who meets the fellow Cretan Meriones as he comes from the battle to retrieve a spear. Idomeneus takes the opportunity to deliver a speech on bravery and cowardice, as if Homer never feels the need for urgency.

It is hard to see how Homer envisions the disposition of troops in this great battle, because only one gate was broken, where Hector attacked and the two Ajaxes defended. Yet the Trojan line seems divided into three parts – two wings and a center – though we never hear anything about the Trojan right wing. Idomeneus and Meriones go to the wing on the Trojan left and kill many, some of them important. Idomeneus briefly comes up against the great Aeneas, with whom he duels inconclusively. The Trojan Helenus, an archer like Paris, and the Trojan Deiphobus are wounded and withdraw. In the complex dance of death, Homer feeds his audience's taste for imaginative gore and gives the world its first description of a "gut-shot," the worst way to die (as every gunfighter knows):

> Adamas shrank back into the throng of his comrades, avoiding fate. But Meriones followed after him as he went and cast with his spear, and hit him midway between his genitals and the navel, where most of all Ares is cruel to wretched mortals. Even there he fixed his spear and the other, leaning over the shaft which pierced him, writhed as a bull that herdsmen amid the mountains have bound with twisted cords and drag with them by force. Even so, when he was hit, he writhed a little while, but not for long. (*Il.* 13.566–73)

Somewhat later, Menelaus smashes the bones of a man's face so thoroughly that his eyes pop out and fall to the ground (13.617)!

The achievements of Idomeneus on the Trojan left wing, together with the stubborn resistance of the two Ajaxes to Hector in the center of the line, lead the prophet Polydamas to urge Hector to pull back. It was Polydamas who earlier interpreted the omen of the eagle and the still-living snake. Hector inspects the left wing and harshly, as often, criticizes his brother Paris, then returns to the center where the battle renews. Hector prepares to go up against Ajax son of Telamon. In military terms, nothing has changed since Hector smashed the gate. Homer has with great versatility delayed the action. Where is Achilles and where is Patroclus all this time? We wonder.

"Deception of Zeus" (Book 14)

To give depth to his delay of the action, and to make plausible the vigor of the Achaean resistance, Homer presents a sequence of scenes that take place at the same time as the "Battle at the Ships," according to a convention of epic verse-making that simultaneous events are reported in sequence. At the end of the "Battle at the Ships" Hector faces off against Ajax; at the end of the "Deception of Zeus," again he faces Ajax. Homer picks up where he left off.

Only now does Nestor come out of his tent, alerted by the sound of battle. He quickly arms, sets off, and immediately encounters the cohort of captains wounded earlier in the fighting, Agamemnon, Diomedes, and Odysseus, all three leaning on their spears as if they were old men, a pathetic sight. The despairing and boorish Agamemnon suggests, for the third time in the poem, that they cut and run, but Odysseus shuts him up with a brusque lecture: if they run, the men at the wall will lose heart and be murdered. Diomedes has the right solution. Though wounded, they should go back and fight. The disguised Poseidon, who has wandered through the ranks rousing the Achaeans to battle for the ships, appears at their side.

Meanwhile, life in heaven continues in a lighthearted vein. Zeus' inattention at the beginning of the "Battle at the Ships" was never explained, but is now intensified by Hera, who favors Poseidon's efforts. Homer's comic vision is strong as he shifts from the gruesome deaths of many and the warrior's grim fate to the halls of heaven. To make sure that Zeus remains in the dark about Poseidon's intention to help the Achaeans, Hera devises an impossible plan: she will seduce her own husband!

In a vigorous parody of the arming scene, Homer describes how Hera makes up at her toilet. Lubriciously she anoints her flesh, which Zeus would ordinarily have little interest in touching. She will need still more help, though, and gets it from her sister Aphrodite, a love amulet in the form of a sash. She bribes the great god Sleep, too, to join her.

In a hilarious scene Zeus takes one look at the new-made goddess and has only one thought. To persuade Hera of the intensity of his sexual desire, he gives a quick catalogue of some of the many, many women by whom he has betrayed her:

> But for the two of us, come, let us take our joy couched together in love, for never yet did desire for goddess or mortal woman so shed itself about me and overmaster the heart in my breast – no, not when I was seized with love for the wife of Ixion, who bore Peirithous, peer of the gods in counsel; nor for Danae of the fair ankles, daughter of Acrisius, who gave birth to Perseus, preeminent above all warriors; nor for the daughter of

far famed Phoenix, who bore for me Minos and godlike Rhadamanthys; nor for Semele, nor for Alcmene in Thebes, who brought forth Heracles, her son strong of heart, and Semele bore Dionysus, the joy of mortals; nor for Demeter, the fair-tressed queen; nor for glorious Leto; no, nor yet for even yourself as now I love you and sweet desire takes hold of me. (*Il.* 14.314–28)

As Zeus and Hera make love atop Mount Ida, flowers spring up around them. Historians of religion connect this description with fertility cults, because Zeus is the sky god and Hera is like the earth, as if their union were that of primordial Sky and Earth. But Homer's interests are entirely humorous. Homer relieves the blood-and-guts butchery and the fulsome self-promotion of his mortal heroes by the bawdy laughter that an all-male monogamist audience would enjoy.

Once Zeus is seduced and subdued by Sleep, Poseidon is free to do what he chooses (that is, he behaves as already described in the "Battle at the Ships"). In the duel between Ajax and Hector, to which we now return, Ajax smashes Hector with a rock, and all Zeus' efforts to fulfill the promise to Thetis have, for the moment, come to nothing. Only by Zeus' will can the Trojans gain the upper hand. And Zeus is fast asleep!

"Fire at the Ships" (Book 15)

Zeus is furious when he awakes and beholds Poseidon's behavior and his wife's part in it. Delighting Homer's audience with portraits of the male's irresistible power, Zeus describes his earlier rough treatment of Hera, when she stepped out of line:

Do you not remember when you were hung from on high, and from your feet I suspended two anvils, and about your wrists I cast a band of gold that might not be broken? And in the air amid the clouds you did hang, and the gods were indignant throughout high Olympus, but they were unable to come close and let you go? (*Il.* 15.18–22)

Hera swears an unbreakable oath that it is "all Poseidon's doing." Zeus has made his point and in a more moderate tone instructs that Iris and Apollo intervene to reverse this unpleasant state of affairs.

In the *Iliad* Zeus never does use violence against other gods, although they plot against him constantly. Asserting his authority, and explaining his behavior, Zeus now summarizes the plot of the *Iliad* in terms that

Homer himself held in his own head as he lazily spun out 16,000 lines of verse:

> Let Hector drive the Achaeans back once more, when he has roused in them craven panic. So will they flee and fall among the many-benched ships of Achilles, son of Peleus, and he will send forth his comrade Patroclus, although glorious Hector will kill him with the spear before the face of Ilios, after Patroclus has killed many others, and among them also my son, good Sarpedon. And in anger for Patroclus will good Achilles kill Hector. Then from that time forth I will cause a driving back of the Trojans from the ships more and more until the Achaeans will take steep Ilios through the devising of Athena. But until that hour neither do I hold back my anger, nor will I allow any other of the immortals to bring aid to the Danaans here, until the desire of the son of Peleus be fulfilled, as I promised at the first and nodded my head thereto, on the day when the goddess Thetis clasped my knees, asking me to do honor to Achilles, sacker of cities. (*Il.* 15.61–77)

In his explanation Zeus yields to Hera, because he agrees that in the end, yes, Troy will fall, just as she desires. Zeus for all his power cannot change what is destined to be.

But the disagreeable Hera has not finished with her blustering husband, and when she returns to Olympus she stirs up the other gods and so angers Ares, because of the death of a son, that Ares prepares to go to the plain and enter the battle. Athena, who thinks that Zeus means what he says, stops him. The messenger Iris receives no welcome greeting either when she tells Poseidon to desist. Poseidon's understanding of the aboriginal division of power places him as equal with Zeus and with Hades, each ruling a third of the world, he protests. Zeus' ascendancy is no more guaranteed constitutionally than is Agamemnon's. Nonetheless, Poseidon chooses, this once, not to press the point.

The healing god Apollo revives Hector and holding the terrible and magical *aegis* before him, a device usually associated with Zeus or Athena, he turns back the Achaeans toward the ships. The *aegis*, which seems to mean "goat-skin," may be in origin a primitive shield and in classical art is shown with snakes as tassels and a Gorgon's head on it. Homer doesn't want to describe again an elaborate attack on the wall, so with a wave of his hand Apollo smashes down a portion of the parapet. By decree the battle everywhere goes to the Trojans (although if you count heads, two Trojans are killed for every Achaean). Homer reminds us that Patroclus is still on his way to Achilles' tent.

In furious fighting the Achaeans fall back to the ships and greater Ajax son of Telamon mounts a ship and with a 30-foot long ship-fighting pike keeps away the Trojans bearing fire, killing 12 with deft strokes. But surely fire is coming to the ships.

"Death of Patroclus" (Book 16)

Patroclus, overwrought because of the army's plight, criticizes Achilles bitterly for allowing anger to ruin his compassion. Achilles admits as much, but is helpless before this overriding emotion:

> Dread grief comes to heart and soul when a man wishes to humiliate his equal and take back the *geras* he has won because he surpasses him in power. Dread grief is this to me, for I have suffered anguish in my heart. The girl that the sons of the Achaeans chose out for me as a *geras*, and that I won with my spear when I had laid waste a well-walled city, her has lord Agamemnon taken back from my arms, this son of Atreus, as though I were some alien who had no rights. (*Il.* 16.52–9)

His character returns with incandescent brilliance as the moral absolutist who *has* been wronged but who will not settle, who fantasizes a world where every Trojan and every Achaean might be dead, and just the two of them remain:

> For I wish, O father Zeus and Athena and Apollo, that no man of the Trojans might escape death, of all that there are, nor any of the Argives, but that the two of us might escape destruction, that alone we might loose the sacred diadem of Troy. (*Il.* 16.97–100)

He will not return, but he will not oppose Nestor's plan. In his confusion Achilles does not see that he has abandoned his resolve never to give in until Agamemnon tastes the full bitterness of defeat. He said to Ajax in the "Embassy to Achilles" that he would return when fire reached the ships, but he will not. He tries to have it two ways – to stick to his resolve to make Agamemnon and his henchmen suffer, and yet to bend before his friend's supplication and the army's need. He describes the disrespect shown to him only because he is tempted to look past the harm he has felt. Allowing Patroclus to go to battle as a substitute violates Achilles' resolve, endangers his friend, and further imperils Achilles' own *timê*, should Patroclus be too successful: hence Achilles warns Patroclus only to drive back the Trojans, then to return. Torn between anger and sympathy, Achilles makes a decision that can only bring catastrophe as his life spins out of control.

Patroclus puts on Achilles' arms (except for the spear, which only Achilles can carry). The original intention was to frighten the Trojans by making them think that Achilles has returned, but Homer drops this ploy and simply shows Patroclus in a splendid *aristeia*. He kills many, pens up the Trojans, and throws others into the ditch before the wall. He comes up against the great Sarpedon, leader of the Lycians, a son to Zeus himself and companion to Glaucus (who gave his gold armor to Diomedes because their ancestors were guest-friends). A sorrowful Zeus considers saving Sarpedon, a minor hero, against fate, but Hera reminds him that she would do the same, and soon anything could happen. Their conversation is not so much a revelation about Fate in Greek thought as a description of the demands of the story. "Fate" is the plot as far as Homer is concerned, and for the plot's sake Sarpedon must die.

Throughout the battle narratives Homer faces the problem of glorifying his fighters while not killing off the very men whose death would bring glory. Remarkably, only two major heroes die in the poem: Patroclus and Hector. Sarpedon, at least, must die if Patroclus is to be glorified. Zeus sends down the gods Sleep and Death to carry Sarpedon's naked despoiled body back to Lycia (the south central coast of modern Turkey), the subject of illustrated vases during the Classical Period.

Patroclus' time has come and the mysterious Apollo himself pushes back Patroclus from the walls of Troy, which Patroclus – possessed by *atê* – for a moment threatened. Apollo strikes Patroclus and his armor flies away, leaving him naked, surrounded by Trojans. A Trojan spears him in the back and Hector finishes him off with a cut to the stomach. Achilles had told Patroclus not to go up against the walls of Troy, which Apollo loves, where Hector is strongest, but Patroclus forgot. The glory of Patroclus' death does not even belong to Hector: he was third to get in a blow. Nevertheless, he will pay the price for Patroclus' death.

"Battle over the Corpse of Patroclus" (Book 17)

Achilles did not accept the terms of the embassy because Agamemnon's offer, though extravagant, was not humble. Achilles then questioned the moral basis for heroic behavior, polluted as it was by Agamemnon's actions. Sending forth Patroclus was a poor compromise. If Patroclus won, and killed Hector, then Achilles would lose his chance for glory; if Patroclus was killed, that would be worse. As Phoenix predicted in the "Embassy," when one refuses Prayers, then Zeus sends *Atê* and the fruits of *Atê* are disaster.

Patroclus' dead and naked body (which Hector nonetheless somehow despoils of Achilles' armor) lies exposed on the plain and over it evolves a complex and bloody struggle to carry the body back to the camp or to Troy, where it can be abused. Homer deftly manages to allow Hector to capture the armor, but not the body. The Trojan capture of Patroclus' body would ruin the story, because then it could be traded back for Hector's body, whose ransom and release form the climax and final resolution in the poem. Yet Hector must put on Achilles' armor, to symbolize his own *atê* and irrevocable destruction.

Many scholars believe that this scene was first evolved in the epic tradition to describe the fight over the body of Achilles, but because Homer does not include Achilles' death in his story, he has adapted it here for other needs. Such a critical approach to Homer is called neo-analysis, a search for earlier unattested oral songs lurking behind the text that is preserved to us. We know from accounts later than the *Iliad* that Achilles killed a great warrior named Memnon, king of Ethiopia. Shortly thereafter Paris killed Achilles with the aid of Apollo. In our *Iliad*, Patroclus, standing in for Achilles, kills Sarpedon, an ally to the Trojans just as was Memnon, then is himself killed through Apollo's agency. Homer has kept the pattern, but changed the names. The fact that Patroclus is wearing Achilles' armor underlines the resemblance. Eerily, Achilles' divine horses weep inconsolably when Patroclus dies – behavior more appropriate to the death of Achilles.

The elaborate fighting over Patroclus' body takes the form of a suc-cession of repeated patterns of narrative. One warrior reproves another for holding back, and the reproved warrior leads a charge. This pattern appears five times. In another pattern one man calls out for help and is answered. So Menelaus calls out for help to Ajax son of Telamon, then to other Achaean leaders, and finally at Ajax's suggestion he calls out to Achilles through the intermediary Antilochus, a son of Nestor. And so Antilochus leaves the field.

The narrative is interlarded with one simile after another, most com-paring the ravages of war to the depredations of animals or their hunting by other animals and humans. At last Menelaus and Meriones get up the naked body, while the two Ajaxes hold back Hector and his Trojans.

"Shield of Achilles" (Book 18)

Achilles already feared that Patroclus was dead, but when Antilochus reports the fact, he is stupefied with grief. Antilochus reports the bare facts, that Patroclus is dead, that they are fighting over his body, and that Hector has the armor.

Achilles says nothing: no words can reveal his grief. He falls to the ground in eloquent despair. His divine mother hears his cry in the depth of the sea, and in his complaint he reveals to Thetis that he understands the plot of his life and that his story is about the destructive power of anger, so sweet to the taste:

Profitless burden on the earth – I that in war am such as no other of the bronze-coated Achaeans, although in council others are better – so may strife perish from among gods and men, and anger that causes a man to grow angry, no matter how wise he might be, and that sweeter far than trickling honey swells like smoke in the breasts of men, even as just now the king of men, Agamemnon, has moved me to anger. (*Il.* 18.104–11)

Achilles agrees to give up his anger against Agamemnon, but only to transfer it to Patroclus' killer, who cannot now escape. Achilles' motives have changed. Before enraged by injustice, he now lusts for revenge. But Achilles' sorrow for Patroclus will become the sorrow of Thetis. She knows that the chain of events unleashed will end in Achilles' death. Mother and son are united in sorrow, the one thing all humans hold in common.

At least Thetis can bring back from Hephaestus a new set of divine armor to replace the armor that Hector took, which also was divine, inherited from Peleus, who got it from Hephaestus. While she travels to Olympus, the battle continues on earth over Patroclus' body. Earlier, Apollo intervened directly for the Trojans when he struck Patroclus on the back and the divine armor flew away. Now Athena intercedes for the Achaeans and casts her *aegis* around Achilles, a golden cloud around his head, and his body blazes like gleaming fire. In a bizarre scene looking forward to even more fantastic events, Achilles stands on the mound behind the camp and three times shouts so loud that "in that hour perished 12 men of their best amid their own chariots and their own spears" (18.230). The Trojans are so unnerved that the Achaeans move in and take the body of Patroclus as the sun sets. They carry it to Achilles' camp, where slave girls clean it and pour out lament, and Achilles swears revenge over it.

In an utter change of mood and setting Thetis enters the charm and mystery of the house of Hephaestus on Olympus, where he creates the most wonderful shield the world has seen, which we discussed above as a representation of Homer's own world (pp. 42–3). Homer's description of the shield inspired many imitators, where in an *ekphrasis* (an elaborate "aside") a poet describes a physical object with such vividness as to create a separate or parallel world. Homer says that Hephaestus is molding bronze, but with 20 bellows to create high temperatures Homer must be thinking of the iron-maker's workshop of his own day.

Dirty and lame, a social outcast, Hephaestus is the soul of courtesy as he breaks from his labor to entertain Thetis, grateful to return a favor. Once, he says, she cared for him when his mother threw him from heaven for being lame (but near the beginning of the *Iliad* (1.590–4) Hephaestus says that *Zeus* threw him from heaven, the only example of conflicting versions of a myth in Homer).

Many have tried to reconstruct the shield's appearance and artists have drawn it, but Homer's description is vague. It is round and has five layers, probably divided into quadrants. Homer must be thinking of metalwork he has seen. The Near Eastern origin of Homer's model seems assured by the Near Eastern artistic convention whereby kings and gods are shown in greater scale than common mortals:

> The rest were faring forth, led by Ares and Pallas Athena, both fashioned in gold, and of gold was the clothing they wore. Handsome were they and tall in their bearing, as is appropriate to gods, clear to view amid the rest, and the folk at their feet were smaller. (*Il.* 18.516–19)

Hephaestus' shield is magical, Homer's best example of a precious and highly wrought physical object. The things and people on it are alive and move like the magical wheeled tripods in Hephaestus' ante-room, which like androids come when you call. The shield is like the cosmos and Hephaestus its creator. There is earth, heaven, sea, sun, moon, constellations upon it. In Egypt the craftsman god Ptah, with whom the Greeks equated Hephaestus, was the creator of the universe.

Freed from the need to establish epic distance, there is no mythical content to events on the shield. In the city at peace, a dispute is resolved, although we can't understand its terms. In the city at war, an enemy besieges a city while the city-dwellers launch an ambush. On another part of the shield is lowland and reaping and a vineyard with winemaking and herds of cattle. Around it all runs the river Ocean that bounds the created world, as everyone knows.

"Agamemnon's Apology" (Book 19)

The death of Patroclus is plot point two, bringing Achilles back into the action so that he can kill Hector and thereby seal his own doom. Before we can enter the poem's final great *aristeia*, which we have awaited so long, Achilles needs to conclude a pact of friendship with Agamemnon and abandon his anger – against him:

> Would that amid the ships Artemis had shot down Briseis with an arrow on the day when I took her from the spoil after I had laid waste Lyrnessus! Then would not so many Achaeans have bitten the huge earth with their teeth beneath the hands of the enemy because of the ferocity of my anger. For Hector and the Trojans was this the better, but long shall the Achaeans, I think, remember the strife between me and you. However, these things will we let be as past and done, for all our pain, curbing the heart in our breasts because we must. Now truly I make my anger to cease. It is not right that I be angry forever without cease. (*Il.* 19.59–68)

Agamemnon insists on presenting the gifts he earlier offered, and Odysseus agrees: only by proper ritual can society's rules be preserved, however much Achilles is aloof with grief and indifferent to them, as he even wishes that Briseis, whom Agamemnon never touched, had died. To him she is now just a woman who caused an unnecessary quarrel and the death of his friend.

Achilles is brusque and to the point in the renunciation of his anger, but in a longwinded apology Agamemnon explains how he never wanted any of this to happen. It was all the fault of *ate*, who did it. To prove the power of *atê*, he tells a myth. Once Hera tricked Zeus so that his beloved son Heracles, whom Hera hated, fell under the power of the tyrannical Eurystheus. Blaming the result on *atê*, called his oldest daughter, Zeus cast her from heaven.

The gifts are brought forward for all to admire. Although Achilles refuses food, Odysseus insists that the others be given a chance to eat. Achilles reveals for the first time that he has a son, Neoptolemus, on the island of Skyros (east of Euboea), who never appears in the *Iliad* but who has an important role in stories about the sack of Troy and its aftermath. Achilles dons his new armor, made by a god but unable to save his life. Even his fairytale horses predict his eventual death, until the Erinyes (who guarantee the natural order, including the separation of humans and animals) tell them to shut up.

"Glory of Achilles" (Book 20)

Achilles' return to battle begins the resolution to the plot in which his war with the world will come to an end. Homer might have had Achilles storm onto the plain, run down Hector, and kill him, but he wants instead to delay the action, to defer the great moment. He also wants to show Achilles routing the whole Trojan army, not just killing its leader.

We have seen a lot of fighting, but the fighting is going to be bigger and better than ever. Homer dramatizes the enormity of the impending conflict by having Zeus invite all the gods, including the rivers and nymphs, to participate in the fight, according to their lights. Homer divides the gods curiously. Most go to the Achaean side: Hera, Athena, Poseidon, Hermes, Hephaestus; but the Trojans get Ares, who is after all the god of war, and of course Phoebus Apollo, thus his sister Artemis too and their mother Leto (who otherwise is almost never mentioned by Homer). Looking ahead to the "Battle with the River," the river Xanthus comes in for the Trojans.

This, the last battle of the poem, parallels the "Glory of Diomedes," the first battle of the poem, with Achilles taking the place of Diomedes. In both battles the gods are present. Apollo, disguised as a mortal, urges Aeneas, the son of Aphrodite, to take on Achilles, now a killing machine storming across the plain at the head of the Achaeans. Aeneas meets the challenge and casts but misses. Achilles throws through the edge of Aeneas' shield and is about to kill him when Aeneas disappears in a cloud of dust, borne away by Poseidon (as Apollo saved Aeneas in his duel with Diomedes). Fate decreed that Aeneas survive the Trojan War and that his descendants rule in the Troad (the area around Troy), as Poseidon says to the other gods:

> Come, let us head him forth out of death so that the son of Cronus will not be angry if Achilles kills him, for it is fated that he escape, that the race of Dardanus [the Trojans] perish not without seed and be seen no more – Dardanus whom the son of Cronus loved above all the children born to him from mortal women. For at last has the son of Cronus come to hate the race of Priam, and now truly will the mighty Aeneas be king among the Trojans, and his sons' sons that shall be born in days to come. (*Il.* 20.300–8)

On this passage was based the immensely influential legend of Aeneas' founding of Rome, inspiring the story that Vergil used to build his great *Aeneid* 800 years after Homer. Many have thought that Homer refers to a real dynasty that claimed descent from Aeneas and ruled the Troad in Homer's day, but there is no direct evidence.

After killing many, Achilles finds Hector, but Apollo spirits him away. Homer wishes to defer still longer the killing of Hector, until Achilles has demonstrated more fully why Agamemnon should have paid him more respect in the first place. Also, we enjoy the mayhem. This is the third time that a god spirits away a hero in a mist, which we saw first in the "Duel between Menelaus and Paris."

"Battle with the River" (21.1–382) and "Battle of the Gods" (21.383–513)

Achilles divides the Trojans in halves, driving one half toward the city while the other half tumbles into the waters of the river Scamander, also called Xanthus ("ruddy"). Yet before this the river has not been prominent in the topology of the battlefield. Achilles stomps through the shallows, putting everyone to the sword. He meets Lycaon, a son of Priam and half-brother of Hector. Achilles had captured him before and ransomed him. When Lycaon begs for life this time, Achilles reminds him that all must die – Patroclus for example, a better man than Lycaon – then plunges his sword into Lycaon's neck. We see Achilles' hate and his intellectual absolutism: he has fashioned a philosophic basis for his pitiless behavior, as have many determined killers throughout history.

Achilles throws the young man's corpse in the Xanthus, setting off one of the oddest, most imaginative sequences in ancient literature. All rivers have spirits, or are spirits, in Homer's religion, and in the "Glory of Achilles" we saw how in the division of the gods Xanthus came in on the Trojan side. The scene is a surreal panorama of exaggerated situations. So many corpses fill the river that they catch in the branches of a downed tree and dam the river so that it rises up and attacks Achilles, nearly drowning him. Miraculously he is saved when Hephaestus, committed to the Achaean side, dries up the waters with his fiery blast. The fantastic mood of the scene separates us from the cold murder of Lycaon and is a preliminary to the big fight to come. Achilles is a mortal, but the "Battle with the River," as with the earlier building of the wall before the camp, may owe its roots to mythical accounts of primeval events, when the world was made in the opposition between water and fire. The story of a hero against the destroying and obliterating waters is very old, attested in a Near Eastern poem from Ugarit of around 1400 BC in which the great god El fights and overcomes Yam, the primeval waters.

Achilles' fight with the river, which brings about Hephaestus' fight with Xanthus, leads to a full-fledged "Battle of the Gods," where the foes earlier assembled attack in earnest. Hera goes against Ares in a comic scene utterly removed from the grim work of slaughter and the aura of cosmic danger we witnessed in Achilles' struggle at the stream. Homer's audience will laugh at Athena acting like Ajax and picking up a big rock to "kapow" the very god of war after he attacks her with a spear:

> So saying he struck her tasseled *aegis* – the awful *aegis* against which not even the lightning of Zeus can prevail – blood-stained Ares struck it with his long spear. She gave ground and seized with her strong hand a stone that lay on the plain, black and jagged and great, that men of former days had set to be the boundary mark of a field. With it she struck furious Ares on the neck and loosed his limbs. Over seven acres he stretched in his fall and befouled his hair with dust and about him his armor clanged. But Pallas Athena broke into a laugh and boasting over him she spoke winged words, "Fool, not even yet have you learned how much stronger than you am I, that you would match your strength with mine. And so you shall satisfy to the full the Avengers invoked by your mother, who in her anger plans evil against you because you have deserted the Achaeans and bear aid to the proud Trojans. (*Il.* 21.400–14)

Athena also smashes Aphrodite in the breast (where it hurts a lot). Apollo refuses to tangle with Poseidon, so that his sister Artemis upbraids him until the obnoxious Hera shows who is boss:

> At that she caught both the other's [Artemis'] hands by the wrist with her left hand and with her right took the bow and its gear from her shoulders and with these weapons, smiling the whole time, she beat her about the ears as she turned this way and that, and the swift arrows fell from out of the quiver. (*Il.* 21.489–92)

A battle between divine beings can only be a mockery.

"Death of Hector" (21.514–22)

Sometimes the worlds of men and gods intersect, and now Achilles pursues Apollo across the plain, thinking he is chasing Agenor, a Trojan noble. When Apollo reveals his trick, Achilles turns back toward the city. Priam sees him, shining like the Dog Star, brilliant, a harbinger of evil. In a speech longwinded and self-pitying Priam begs Hector to come inside. The death of Hector is the death of Troy, and Priam imagines the horror of his own death:

> Ravening dogs will rend me last, when they come in my door after some man by thrust or throw of sharp bronze has robbed my limbs of life – the very dogs that in my halls I reared at my table to guard my door. Having drunk my blood in the madness of their hearts they shall lie there in the gateway. A young man looks good when he is killed in battle and he lies mangled by the sharp bronze. Though he is dead, all is honorable, though you can see every part of him. But when dogs work shame on the white head and white beard and on the nakedness of a dead old man, this is the most piteous thing that comes on wretched mortals. (*Il.* 22.66–76)

Hector's mother Hecuba bears her breasts – he sucked from these and he owes her something. Hector's mind is racing. Should he go inside and lose *timê*? Should he try to make a deal with Achilles, give back Helen and the loot? What if Achilles cuts him down like a woman? Already it is too late for Hector. Achilles is upon him. The great Trojan loses his nerve and runs, his bravery overcome by fear. Achilles now earns his epithet "swift-footed." In front a good man flees, who has much to protect and a lot to lose, but one mightier by far is in pursuit, armed by the gods and dedicated to revenge. "It was not for beast of sacrifice or for bull's hide that they strove, such as are men's prizes for swiftness of foot, but it was for the life of horse-taming Hector that they ran" (22.159–62).

Achilles chases Hector down the wagon track past the two springs: one hot even in winter when it steams, and one icy cold even in summer. Modern explorers have looked in vain for these springs, but they are literary symbols of the land at peace, when Trojan maids washed their clothes in them. Now it is war and Troy is about to lose its finest son. Three times they run around the walls of Troy. (The ruins at Hissarlik, taken to be Troy, are actually on a promontory.)

When Patroclus died, Apollo first struck him so that his armor fell away. Now Athena takes the form of Hector's brother Deiphobus and tricks Hector into a fight he cannot win. When Deiphobus disappears in a puff, Hector knows he is doomed. We the audience have known that from the beginning. Achilles spears Hector through the throat but misses the vocal chords, so that Hector can still beg for an honorable burial. Achilles explains he would prefer to eat his flesh. At least he can treat his body shamefully. And Hector dies.

Priam and Hecuba, looking on from the wall, collapse, but the good wife Andromache is in her room weaving. She hears a cry and runs to the wall to see her husband dragged behind Achilles' chariot, his long dark hair spread out behind him.

> Then down over her eyes came the darkness of night and enfolded her and she fell backward and gasped forth her spirit. Far from off her head she cast its bright attiring, the frontlet and cap and kerchief and woven band, and the veil that golden Aphrodite had given her on the day when Hector of the flashing helm led her as his bride forth from the house of Eetion after he had brought bride-gifts past counting. (*Il.* 22.466–72)

Andromache's veil is her virtue, the sexual bond between her and Hector that will soon be violated when the city is taken and the women given to rape. To cast aside the veil is to give herself to rape, as to "tear the veil" of a city means to destroy it: the same word in Greek (*krêdemnon*) means "veil" and "battlement." We too speak of the "rape of a city." Andromache describes the sorry future that must await their half-orphaned child, but we know it will be far worse.

"Ghost of Patroclus" (23.1–107) and "Funeral of Patroclus" (23.108–897)

Achilles will not wash until Patroclus is buried. That night the *psyché* or ghost of Patroclus appears to Achilles in a dream, a sequence for which a clear parallel is found in the Near Eastern *Gilgamesh* poem, when the ghost of the dead Enkidu appears to Gilgamesh and begs to be buried. The Homeric passage is a *locus classicus* for our understanding of the Homeric concept of the *psyché*, really the breath that leaves a body at death (*psyché* = "breath-soul," plural = *psychai*):

> Bury me as soon as possible so that I might pass within the gates of Hades. The *psychai* keep me aloof at a distance, the phantoms of men who are done with toils, nor will they allow me to join them beyond the river, but vainly I wander through the wide-gated house of Hades. (*Il.* 23.71–4)

The *psyché* cannot be "laid" – got rid of, sent into the other world – until buried and suffers when adrift in an in-between world. Having the same form as in life, the *psyché* is nevertheless insubstantial, and when Achilles reaches out to touch it, "the *psyché* like a vapor was gone beneath the earth, gibbering faintly" (23.100–1). A similar scene appears in the *Odyssey* when Odysseus tries to touch the *psyché* of his mother, but cannot, and Vergil imitates it when he shows Aeneas in the underworld reaching out to a shadowy Dido (*Aeneid* 6.472–3).

Achilles does not disobey. He burns Patroclus' body on a pyre decorated by the gory sacrifice of many men and animals. The pyre burns and the bones are gathered. Proving again his devotion to a slow narrative pace, Homer shifts his tone utterly in the funeral games for Patroclus, the world's oldest sports reporting, in which many have seen Homer's most refined artistry.

Unlike games in the Classical Period, here every contestant wins a prize. The prizes tell us something about what was valued in the Homeric economy. For example, in one contest the loser gets a woman, worth four oxen! The eight events are chariot racing, boxing, wrestling, footracing, armed combat, shot put, archery, and javelin. The chariot race is the longest and most complex, taking half the length of the entire games. Even the gods are involved: Athena intervenes to restore to Diomedes his whip when he drops it. The gentlemanly mood of the funeral games, as against the savagery and gloom that has gone before, is clear when Antilochus offers a second prize to Menelaus and Menelaus hands it back to him. Achilles, in perfect control of his emotions and exemplary director of the games, gives a prize to Agamemnon without competition, saying that Agamemnon is "supreme in power," thus placing a cap on their formal reconciliation.

"Ransom of Hector" (Book 24)

After burying Patroclus, Achilles is desolate, his exaggerated behavior always just short of madness. He thinks on the good times they once shared, walks the beach at night, and in the morning drags the useless corpse of Hector through the dust in a gorgeous image of the uselessness of mortal flesh. Achilles can never be healed, and there is no sanctity in revenge. Patroclus has received his fine burial, nearly compensation for death itself; Hector, by contrast, is a mutilated corpse (though Apollo won't allow it to decay). Still, Achilles' grief is not assuaged. The gods wish to end the outrage and consider sending Hermes, god of thieves, to steal the body. In this context Homer gives us the only reference in the Homeric poems to the famous story of the Judgment of Paris (though we'd like to know why Poseidon is included):

> And the thing was pleasing to all the rest, but not to Hera or Poseidon or the flashing-eyed maiden [Athena], but they continued even as when at the first sacred Ilios became hateful in their eyes and Priam and his people, because of the sin of Alexander [Paris] who put reproach on those goddesses when they came to his steading and preferred her who furthered his fatal lustfulness. (*Il.* 24.25–30)

Zeus summons Thetis, who will advise Achilles to give up the body for burial. The messenger goddess Iris goes to Priam and tells him he must journey to Achilles' tent, bearing ransom for the body of his son. Achilles, however, is through his own understanding coming to the end of his anger, first directed against Agamemnon, then against Hector. In reply to his mother's request he says simply:

> So let it be. Whoever brings ransom, let him bear away the dead, if truly with eagerness of heart the Olympian himself so bids. (*Il.* 24.139–40)

We have seen little of Hermes in this poem. He enters in the "Battle of the Gods" against Leto, but they decide not to engage. In classical Greek religion Hermes joins this world to the next, and many have noticed how the "Ransom of Hector" appears to be based on a *katabasis* ("down-going"), an old mythical story about descent to the underworld. As Priam creeps through the darkness across the plain, he comes to a river (Patroclus begs to be allowed to cross the river into the other world). There Hermes meets him, disguised as a Myrmidon. Hermes takes the reins, and when they come to the ramparts, a strange sweet sleep falls on the eyes of the guards and the gates burst open by themselves. Earlier Achilles' housing is described vaguely as a hut or tent, but now it is a massive fortification with a gigantic bolt that only three ordinary men can move (of course, Achilles can do it alone). Achilles is like the death lord and this is his dwelling. Homer is using the language of *katabasis* to lend solemnity and drama to this final resolution. Priam has come to get a body, led by Hermes, who joins this world to the next. In later myth, Orpheus descends to the underworld to bring back his dead wife Eurydice.

The mythic substructure gives the scene a creepy flavor, but Homer's purpose is to resolve his plot. Achilles rejects the moral basis of heroic behavior in the "Embassy to Achilles," denying the proffered gifts and claiming that his *timê* comes from Zeus. After killing Hector, he spoke with equal intemperance, and in similar terms, when he said he would never give up the body for burial, not if he received as much wealth as was in Troy before the coming of the long-haired Achaeans. Now he *will* give it up, along with his wrath. It is pointless to divide the world into friends and enemies, he sees, when all men, even he and Priam, are united in their suffering. Here is Homer the moral genius, who anticipates the theory of the brotherhood of man later promulgated by Greek philosophers and Christian moralists.

Thanks to Hermes' aid, Priam enters the hut unnoticed:

Unseen great Priam entered in and coming close to Achilles clasped his knees in his hands and kissed his hands, the terrible, man-slaying hands that had killed many sons of his. And as when *atê* comes on a man who in his own country kills another and escapes to a land of strangers, to the house of some man of substance, and wonder holds those who look on him, even so was Achilles seized with wonder at the sight of godlike Priam and seized with wonder were the others too, and they glanced at each other. But Priam made entreaty and spoke to him, saying, "Remember your father, O Achilles like to the gods, whose years are like mine, on the terrible threshold of old age. (*Il.* 24.477–87)

Looking at the old man Achilles does see his own father in him, and at this moment understands:

But come, please take a seat, and our sorrows will we allow to lie quiet in our hearts, despite our pain. No profit comes from cold lament. For the gods have spun the thread for wretched mortals so that they should live in pain while they themselves are without sorrow. Two urns are set on the floor of Zeus of gifts that he gives, the one of evil, the other of blessings. To whom Zeus who hurls the thunderbolt gives a mingled lot, that man meets now with evil, now with good, but to whom he gives only the evil, him he makes to be hated of man and an evil famine drives him over the face of the sacred earth, and he wanders honored not by gods nor by mortals. (*Il.* 24.522–33)

For some, life is wholly bad; for others, there is occasional good, but otherwise bad, an exemplary summary of Greek pessimism. Priam has no patience for this philosophizing and wants to take the body and leave, and in a luminous characterization Achilles' angers flickers back to life. Well, he might kill the old man after all, father to the man who killed his friend, and Priam should keep that in mind.

Then they eat and in their communion of wine and meat their mutual hate and suspicion fall away so that each sees the glory in the other. So ends the anger of Achilles. After 11 days, the Trojans burn and bury Hector. So ends the poem.

Conclusion: The Tragedy of the *Iliad*

"Tragedy" was a genre of poetry performed at the theater of Dionysus in Athens beginning in the late sixth century BC, but in critical parlance it designates a kind of story, of which the *Iliad* is the earliest example. In tragedy a highly individualistic character falls out with the world around him, becomes progressively more isolated, and in the end is completely alone, in or near the ultimate isolation of death. Even so, Achilles finds himself in a quarrel with his superior and his supporters. He indulges his strong feelings based in a sense of justice and refuses to be reconciled with those who have offended him until he has caused harm to someone he loves, when reconciliation loses all meaning. Achilles' anger toward Agamemnon becomes anger toward Hector, whose body he treats barbarically. When Achilles abandons his anger, along with Hector's body, he has a deep moral vision about the universal suffering that unites all humankind, but no one with whom to share it. Soon, we are told repeatedly, he will meet his own death, now a virtual certainty. In the tragedy of the *Iliad* there is no happy resolution to the dilemma that faces all human beings, alive but doomed to die.

5

The *Odyssey*

Everything about the *Odyssey* is different from the *Iliad*. They are literary opposites, long the best argument that both poems are the invention of one man, one of the greatest artists that ever lived. Life is big, life is moral. There is war, there is family. The *Iliad* is about war, the *Odyssey* is about a man trying to get home. On the way he becomes a symbol for the human spirit in quest of the meaning of human life. Not that Odysseus seeks knowledge as such in his wanderings: he doesn't. However, his wandering symbolizes the human quest for knowledge. As the *Iliad* defines the West's preoccupation with the philosophy of value – why should I do anything? – the *Odyssey* defines its restless quest for discovery of new things.

While Odysseus is lost at sea and presumed dead, a clique of over 100 well-born men from Ithaca and neighboring islands have moved into his house, urging Penelope to marry one of them. Each wants to become the next *basileus*, "king" or "Big Man," though we are never sure what that entails beyond control of Odysseus' house and lands. Apparently the widow of the old Big Man (Odysseus) determines through remarriage who will be the next Big Man. In its general setting Homer describes the historical transition from rule by petty kings, the Big Men, in the Iron Age, to rule by aristocratic oligarchies in the early historical period in the eighth century BC. In Homer's story the older generation of the Big Men is triumphant. Homer's audience must have been in the courts of just such men. In the end Odysseus kills every single one of the presumptuous young men who allow amorous inclinations to justify rude behavior.[10]

Whereas the *Iliad* is set in the heroic age, the world of the *Odyssey* (except for Fairyland) is simply Homer's world. Sometimes critics call the *Iliad* a saga, because of its pretense to be set long ago in a world peopled by a greater race, and they call the *Odyssey* a romance, because it describes a contemporary world with allowance for exaggerated effects. Why should the hero's home be the obscure island of Ithaca, to the west of the Greek mainland in the mouth of the Gulf of Corinth? Heinrich Schliemann, confident in the historicity of the Homeric poems, found the ruins of Troy and Mycenae and Tiryns, but on Ithaca he found nothing, nor has intensive later investigation found a Bronze Age palace. But in the age of Western Greek exploration beginning in the late ninth and early eighth centuries BC, Ithaca was directly on the coastal route to Italy. Today, yachts exploring the Mediterranean still put into port on Ithaca before heading north to Corcyra, from where the Italian coast is nearly visible.

Invocation and Prologue: "Crime Never Pays" (1.1–95)

The *Iliad* takes place over a few days in the tenth year of the war. Its story is linear: first the quarrel, then the embassy, then the death of Patroclus, then the burial of Hector. The *Odyssey*, too, has a linear background: Telemachus goes to find his father, his father comes home, they plot, and they kill the suitors. But against this background are spirals and flashbacks that extend the story of the *Odyssey* over ten years and give the *Odyssey* a very different shape from the *Iliad*. Fully one sixth of the poem is Odysseus' famous apologue, "speech" (Books 9–12), a long flashback.

As a general type, the *Odyssey* is a *nostos* ("homecoming," plural *nostoi*) and contains several shorter *nostoi* presented as flashbacks. For example, in Book 4 in a long speech Menelaus describes his adventures while coming home, which sound like a foreshortening of Odysseus' own adventures. In the second half of the poem, after Odysseus returns home, comes a long sequence of "false tales" – fictional accounts of Odysseus' wanderings. Such fictional *nostoi*, like the famous apologue of Books 9–12, stop the progression of the narrative cold while enriching the story by taking us back in time, real or imaginary. The *Iliad*, too, has occasional flashbacks – for example, the telling of the oracle of the snake and the birds (*Il.* 2.303–32) or Nestor's early exploits (*Il.* 11.670–761) – but its structure remains a forceful linear drive from crisis to resolution. The *Odyssey*, by contrast, seeks every opportunity to prolong the story through related tangential tales.

The central theme of the *Iliad* is psychological: the destructive power of anger, that sweet feeling that comes with hate. The central theme of the *Odyssey* is moral: that the evil pay for their deeds, so we need not feel sorry for the suitors cut down in cold blood. Homer announces the moral theme right at the beginning:

> Tell me, O Muse, of the man of many turns, who wandered many ways after he sacked the sacred citadel of Troy. Many were the men whose cities he saw and whose minds he learned, yes, and many the sorrows he felt in his heart upon the sea, seeking to save his own *psychê* and the *nostos* of his comrades. Yet even so he did not save his comrades, although he wished very much to do so, for through their own blind folly they perished – the fools! who devoured the cattle of Helius Hyperion, who took from them the day of their *nostos*. Of these things, goddess, daughter of Zeus, beginning where you wish, tell to us. (*Od.* 1.1–10)

Crime never pays, which is why Odysseus' men died and he survived. They broke the rules, violated the taboo. They ate the cattle of the sun when they were not supposed to, but Odysseus didn't and he survived. He is the "man of many turns" because he is flexible and versatile, and he does what is required. The first word in the poem is *anêr* ("man"), a male of the species, as *mênis* ("anger") is the first word of the *Iliad*. This story is about the adventures of the male (not the female), but he will meet many females on his way. He is not taken for a fool, and he subordinates his behavior to his moral intelligence. His men were fools. They broke the law and they died.

This pattern of basic good and basic evil, clear-cut but simple moral distinctions, is common to traditions of folktale all over the world and in its deep structure the *Odyssey* is a kind of folktale (the *Iliad* is not a folktale). A man is gone for a long time. He comes home just as his wife is about to marry another. At first no one recognizes him, but somehow he proves his identity. He destroys his enemies, reunites with his wife, and lives happily ever after. Whereas the *Iliad*'s theme of the death of a friend followed by regret and scrutiny appears prominently in the Near Eastern *Gilgamesh* epic, Homer's *Odyssey* presents the first known example of this folktale. It is impossible to say where he got it. The ancient Near East provides no good model, although many details are based on Eastern patterns. Of course, entire genres have disappeared from the record of ancient Near Eastern literature; for example, the animal fable clearly attested in artistic representations in Mesopotamia and Egypt. Presumably Homer inherited his story from the mass of folktales that must have been the *aoidos'* stock in trade.

In the *Iliad* Zeus metes out good and evil from the jars before his throne, or Fate is responsible for suffering. In the *Odyssey* Zeus enunciates the theme of human moral responsibility when a council of the gods decrees Odysseus' release from the island of Calypso:

> Look you now, how happy mortals are to blame the gods. It is from us, they say, that evils come, but they by themselves, through their own blind folly, have sorrows beyond that which is allotted. (*Od.* 1.32–4)

Take, for example, the House of Atreus, in the *Odyssey* a paradigm for good and bad behavior. The gods warned Atreus not to sleep with Clytemnestra, Agamemnon's wife, while Agamemnon was at Troy, but he did so anyway. When Agamemnon returned, the adulterous couple murdered him. The price they paid was clear: Orestes, son of Agamemnon and Clytemnestra, came from abroad and killed Aegisthus. On the one hand is Odysseus, his son Telemachus, and his wife Penelope; on the other hand is Agamemnon, his son Orestes, and his wife Clytemnestra. Clytemnestra strayed, Penelope remained true. *Cherchez la femme*, and do not blame the gods for your trouble.

While Zeus sends Hermes to free Odysseus, Athena hastens to Ithaca in disguise.

"Hosting of Mentes/Athena" (1.96–444)

After his moralizing prologue, Homer opens his story in the dark dining halls of Odysseus' palace on Ithaca, where the boorish young bucks drink, whore, and listen to poetry. In the midst of the *grand scandale* appears a mysterious stranger. The story is about to begin.

Mentes, the stranger at the door, is really Athena in disguise. In the *Iliad* many gods are prominent, but in the *Odyssey* only three play important roles: Athena, protectress of the hero; Zeus, protector of the moral law; and Poseidon, persecutor of the hero, who represents the sea and all its real and symbolic dangers. Mentes/Athena is plying the international metals trade, "sailing over the wine-dark sea to men of strange speech, on my way to Temese for copper, and I carry with me shining iron" (*Od.* 1.183–4). The location of Temese is uncertain, but perhaps it is in southern Italy, to where Euboeans sailed in the early eighth century BC to acquire metal ores. Mentes knew Odysseus in the old days before the Trojan War. Could this be the master's child, he wonders, and Telemachus answers:

> My mother says that I am his child, but I don't know, for never yet did any man by himself know his own parentage. I wish I was the son of some fortunate man, whom old age overtook among his own possessions. But, yes, of him who was the most unfortunate of mortal men they say I am sprung, since you ask. (*Od.* 1.215–20)

Literary character is built on dramatic need (what the character wants) and on point of view (how he or she sees the world). Homer, at a stroke, establishes Telemachus' dramatic need – to find his father – and his point of view as a sullen teenager who doubts even his own parentage.

Horrified at what is going on in the house, Mentes/Athena gives Telemachus strong advice about what he must do to restore order. He must expel the greedy suitors, then sail to Pylos on the mainland, then go to Sparta to seek news of his father's whereabouts. Of course Mentes/Athena knows very well where Odysseus is, and Telemachus will in fact learn nothing, but the purpose of the journey is to bring Telemachus out of the world of children and into the world of men. The story of Telemachus is the first example in world literature of what the Germans call a *Bildungsroman*, the story of how a boy grows up and becomes a man. Since the *Odyssey*, the *Bildungsroman* has been a principal story type in Western literature.

Mentes/Athena leaves and the *aoidos* Phemius Terpiades, whose name means the "famous one meant to please," takes up his song. Phemius sings about the return of the Achaeans after the Trojan War – the *Odyssey* is just such a song, the sort of music that Penelope doesn't like! When she boldly enters the den of lustful suitors to complain, Telemachus, seeking his maturity, rebukes her for her taste in music. When it comes to *aoidic* song, you have to go with the times, he says, and these *nostoi* are very popular. Telemachus may be an adolescent without power in his home, but his interview with Mentes/Athena has already made him boss of his own mother.

"Assembly of the Ithacans" and "Departure of Telemachus" (Book 2)

With breathtaking speed Homer sets up his plot. Telemachus calls an assembly of all Ithacans and announces that he's fed up with the suitors' depredations and that somebody should do something about it. Apparently anyone has the right to call an assembly, as any *basileus* can in the *Iliad*, but this is the first assembly since Odysseus went to Troy 20 years ago, Homer says, and Odysseus' unprotected property has for a long time been the object of greed and violence.

Deftly, Homer sketches the character of Antinous, a leader of the suitors, who with arrogance accepts Telemachus' charge about their bad behavior, then says it's none of their fault because Penelope, a cunning trickster (like her husband), said she'd marry one of them once she finished weaving a burial shroud for Laertes, Odysseus' aged father. But at night she unwove the shroud – a folktale motif and a story that Homer tells three times in the *Odyssey*. Yet he poorly weaves the motif into his own web, for already three years have passed since Penelope's trick was discovered, but she still has not chosen one of the suitors to marry.

In a sometimes confusing account of marriage customs, Antinous outrageously suggests that Telemachus send Penelope back to her own father, so that she can be remarried and that gifts, dowry (from her parents), and bridal price (from the groom) may be exchanged. Telemachus threatens divine requital against the suitors and an omen from Zeus of two eagles fighting supports his words. Halitherses, an Ithacan noble, predicts Odysseus' return and the death of the suitors, but to the brash, lustful, hungry, and disrespectful suitors there are no limits to bad manners, least of all from the gods. Like Odysseus' men, they are fools who think they are invulnerable. According to the suitor Leocritus,

> If Ithacan Odysseus himself were to come and be eager at heart to drive out from his hall the lordly suitors who are feasting in his house, then should his wife have no joy at his coming, though she longed for him very much, but right here would he meet a shameful death, if he fought with men who outnumbered him. (*Od.* 2.246–51)

In folktales, as in life, pride goes before a fall, and in Book 22 Telemachus will kill Leocritus.

For now the island is in open revolt and Telemachus, caught in the middle, requests a ship to sail in quest of his father. After taking stores from the palace, he escapes that night with Athena's help, who now takes on the form of a certain Mentor (whence our term "mentor" = advisor) and, to recruit sailors, the form of Telemachus himself. Thus, three times Athena appears in bodily form in the opening scenes to assist Telemachus; while Odysseus is lost on the high seas, by contrast, she never appears even once.

"Telemachus in Pylos" (Book 3)

As in a flash the boat with Athena/Mentor, Telemachus, and followers appears on the shore of Pylos, where a great sacrifice is taking place to the god Poseidon, a strong supporter of the Achaeans during the Trojan War and the explicit enemy of Odysseus (because Odysseus blinded his son Polyphemus). About 4,500 Pylians are gathered on the shore to kill 81 bulls, an epic sacrifice, and in its piety and good order the opposite of the situation on Ithaca. Telemachus respectfully asks Nestor if he knows anything about his father.

Nestor sings his own *nostos* and tells all that happened after they left Troy: disagreement between the sons of Atreus, the division of the fleet, his own uneventful return. In Nestor's speech Homer displays a good knowledge of sea-lanes from the Troad to Greece; he must have traveled on them, as must some of his audience. Nestor pities the lot of Telemachus, but is sure that if Athena loves him, as surely she did his father, the suitors will be sorry. Even as he speaks, the disguised Athena stands at Telemachus' side! But the depressed young man replies:

> Old man, in no way do I think that this word will come to pass. Too great is what you say and amazement holds me. I have no hope that this will come to pass, no, not though the gods should will it. (*Od.* 3.226–8)

Athena takes friendly exception to Telemachus' depressing view, adding that it is better to come home late but safe than early and dead, as did Agamemnon, Zeus' paradigm for human moral responsibility.

But why didn't Menelaus avenge his brother's murder, Telemachus wonders. Because he was lost for seven years (a magic number), Nestor says. Now Telemachus must journey inland to visit him, in case Menelaus may know something about Odysseus' whereabouts. When Mentor/Athena flies off as a bird, Telemachus understands who has accompanied him. To honor the goddess, Nestor offers a second sacrifice, a heifer. Homer tells us every detail of the animal's killing, so we understand fairly well what actually happened at a religious rite in early Greece.

"Telemachus in Sparta" (4.1–331), "*Nostos* of Menelaus" (4.332–619), and "Plotting of the Suitors" (4.620–847)

As in a magical journey, Telemachus and Pisistratus, the son of Nestor, make an intermediate stop, then travel by chariot over the Taygetus range separating Messenia in the southwestern Peloponnesus, where Pylos is, from the valley of Lacedaemon in southeastern Peloponnesus, where Sparta is. This would be a rough ride over rugged high mountains, but Homer seems unclear about the real geography of the southern Peloponnesus.

Homer's description of marital tension in Sparta between Helen and Menelaus is a masterpiece of domestic satire and, as sometimes in Homer, modern in tone. Telemachus and Pisistratus come to Sparta on the very day that Hermionê, Helen's only child, and a bastard son of Menelaus are to marry in a double wedding ceremony. Helen had abandoned Hermionê to flee with her sex-mate Paris to Troy, a passionate but infertile union, but now she's back home and all is forgotten. As pious sacrifice distinguished Telemachus' visit in Pylos, so different from the perversions he suffered at home, the young man now experiences the joy of legitimate marriage, so unlike the snake pit on Ithaca. With each example Telemachus travels into the world of good taste and social stability, a fatherless child learning new models of behavior.

The *Odyssey* is obsessed with recognitions, a folktale device. There are none in the *Iliad*, but in the *Odyssey* they follow one after the other. The grand series of recognitions pertains to Odysseus, but Telemachus is his worthy son. He is at first unrecognized in Sparta, but when he sheds tears at the mention of Odysseus, Menelaus suspects and the clever and beguiling Helen knows that this is Telemachus, the son of Odysseus. Helen's recognition is the sign of Telemachus' maturation, and the thought of his noble father, whom Telemachus now so resembles, reduces everyone to sorrow.

Helen produces a powerful drug, *nepenthê* ("no pain"), that she got in Egypt and slips it into the punch bowl. Soon they all feel hilarious. To praise Odysseus, Helen explains how once Odysseus came in disguise to Troy (as he will do on Ithaca), but she recognized him and helped him kill many Trojans. She was always working to her husband's advantage!

To get back at his wife's claims and insinuations, but without spoiling the mood, Menelaus now praises Odysseus too, remembering how he saved the Achaeans on the night when Helen stood outside the Trojan

Horse with Deiphobus, her new husband after Paris' death, and she imitated the voices of the wives of the men hidden inside. Thanks be that Odysseus held his hand over their mouths!

On the next day Menelaus tells the story of his own *nostos* from Troy, one that parallels that of Odysseus, though it is less complex. First he was held up in Egypt, then sailing away was stranded on the island of Pharos, a "full day's journey from the coast" (the real island of Pharos is in the bay of Alexandria a few hundred yards offshore). A sea nymph befriended him, Eidothea, "Divine of Form" (as a sea goddess, Leucothea, will befriend Odysseus). He disguised himself beneath the skin of a seal (as Odysseus will cling beneath a ram to escape from Cyclops). He met a powerful prophetic being, Proteus, Old Man of the Sea, and overcame him (as Odysseus spoke with the prophetic Teiresias on the coast of the land of the Cimmerians). From Proteus, Menelaus learned the sad fate of his brother Agamemnon, and of lesser Ajax, son of Oileus, punished for overconfidence. He also learned that Odysseus was held on the island of Calypso ("concealer") against his will (even so, Odysseus learned from Teiresias of the fates of his companions).

Armed with this meager information, Telemachus departs the next day, endowed with a splendid Phoenician bowl:

> Of all the gifts that lie stored as treasures in my house, I will give you that one which is fairest and costliest. I will give you a well-wrought mixing bowl all of silver and with gold rims, the work of Hephaestus. The warrior Phaedimus, king of the Sidonians, gave it to me when his house sheltered me as I went there, and now I am minded to give it to you. (*Od.* 4.613–19)

Such gifts are of great economic importance in Homeric society. The gift established relationships of *xenia*, as existed between Glaucus and Diomedes in the *Iliad*. On Greek *xenia* was built the international network along which men of high social birth could travel and not be harmed.

Meanwhile, back on Ithaca, the suitors plot to murder Telemachus when he returns. These men are not just bad mannered, lustful, greedy, and oafish, but murderers too. We touch on Ithaca before turning, at plot point one, to the escape of Odysseus from his prison on the high seas.

"Odysseus and Calypso" (Book 5)

Now we return to the very council in heaven where the poem began, and the subsequent action, according to the convention of epic narrative for representing simultaneous action, we understand to take place at the same time as what went before. Athena complains to Zeus about her beloved Odysseus all over again, as she did in Book 1, first impelling Telemachus to action, now doing the same for his father. Just as Athena went to Ithaca disguised as Mentes, Zeus sends Hermes to Calypso's island with instructions to free Odysseus.

Why Hermes? In the *Iliad* Hermes guides Priam's chariot through the night, across the river, and past the sentinels according to a mythical pattern of *katabasis* or descent into the underworld. Athena (busy on Ithaca in any event) has no affinity with the other world. Odysseus is trapped at the "navel of the sea," where this world meets the next. In classical times the shamanistic god Apollo revealed at Delphi (called the "navel") a secret knowledge.

At the level of external plot, it's true that the *Odyssey* is a story about a man who returns home just as his wife is about to marry. At the level of myth or internal structure, however, the *Odyssey* is the story of a man who returns from the dead. In myth, water is the original element from which the world emerged, before anything came to exist. Poseidon, god of water, is Odysseus' enemy. Symbolically, Odysseus on the island of Calypso (= "concealer"), a figure that Homer may have himself invented, is Odysseus in the land of the dead. Death is the great "concealer" (Hades means "unseen"), and in Greek the verb *kaluptô* can mean simply to "bury" a dead body. Calypso wants to hold back Odysseus from his wife and his son and his home. The eternal life that she offers Odysseus, if he will stay, is an eternal death for the man who loves experience and who loves his home. He will be reborn and live again.

Angrily, Calypso attacks the rules that keep mortal men from the arms of goddesses like herself. When she informs Odysseus that he may go, he suspects a trick. Calypso is the ambivalent female who in the folktale both helps the hero and loves him, but wants to hold him back, to harm him.

In the single most difficult passage in Homer, Odysseus builds a "raft" to escape from the island, but Homer seems to be thinking more of a boat because the craft has "ribs" and perhaps "gunwales." Perhaps he has taken traditional language from the building of the Argo in the epic about Jason to which Homer later refers (*Od.* 12.70). Odysseus may be a hero, but unlike the spear-fighters on the windy plain of Troy he can do real things in a real world. Athena his patron is the goddess of just such practical skills, of weaving and carpentry, skills that make a difference in human life.

Poseidon, returning from the blessed Ethiopians, espies Odysseus on the high seas and sends a great storm, and we are given a riveting description of the terror that every sailor knows. No sailor loves the sea, and the dangerous and implacable Poseidon, who favored the Achaeans during the war at Troy, is now the enemy. Nothing external motivates the appearance of Leucothea, who with her strange umbilical-like veil is the female agent that allows Odysseus to escape Poseidon's world, the sea (just as Eidothea made Menelaus' *nostos* possible).

Odysseus is naked, bereft of every worldly thing, helpless, weak, emerged from the primordial element wherein a fetus also lives. As if dead on Calypso's island, he returns to life on Scheria, island of the Phaeacians. Once ashore, assisted by Leucothea, half drowned, Odysseus hides beneath two bushes so tightly woven together that the rain never penetrates them. In a hollow, which Homer compares to a hearth preserving a spark, he sleeps. The scene symbolizes his rebirth. Held captive for seven years, a magical number, he emerges naked from the sea, which is death, but from which life proceeds. The hollow that protects him is a womb. The Greek word for "spark" is *sperma*, which also means "seed."

"Odysseus and Nausicaa" (Book 6) and "Odysseus in the Phaeacian Court" (Book 7)

When reborn, as a "youth" Odysseus seeks a mate and in a situation of extreme delicacy finds one in the charming Nausicaa ("ship-girl"), daughter of King Alcinous ("strong-ship"). Most Phaeacians have "ship" names and, as Nausicaa explains, they are not much good with the bow and arrow either; they are consummate seafarers. We are wary in correlating Odyssean geography with real geography, but already in Thucydides in the fifth century BC Scheria, as the Phaeacians call their island, was identified with Corcyra north of Ithaca off the coast of northwest Greece, the natural jumping off place for sailors faring west to Italy. In history Corcyra was in fact a halfway house between the wild and dangerous west of the Italian peninsula and mainland Greece, home sweet home.

Arrival in Ithaca meant that the sailor had returned. Homer has brilliantly recast historical fact (Ithaca = back in Greece) as the folktale of the man who returned after many years, and as the myth of resurrected life.

In one of his best scenes Homer captures the modesty and courage of the young Nausicaa and the sexual tension natural in her meeting with an older man of wide experience. Inspired by Athena in a dream, ready for marriage, she has come to the seashore with her girlfriends to wash clothes (though she is a princess!); no one wants to wear dirty clothes at a wedding. Earlier, we saw Homer's description of Poseidon; here he formulates the famous image of Artemis with which we are all familiar. He compares Nausicaa among her maids to the goddess:

And even as Artemis the archer roves over mountains along the ridges of high Taygetus or Erymanthus, rejoicing in the chase of boars and swift deer, and the wood nymphs, daughters of Zeus who bears the *aegis*, share her sport, and Leto is glad at heart – high above them all Artemis holds her head and brows and easily may she be known, though all are beautiful – even so amid her handmaids shone the unwed maid. (*Od.* 6.102–8)

Greek *nymphê* can mean simply "a young girl," and in a magical setting on an exotic island Nausicaa and her maids truly are like Artemis and her "nymphs."

The girls play ball, but when a ball goes astray they shout, waking Odysseus. He staggers out among them covered in brine, naked except for a branch he holds, emerged from three days in the sea. The contrast between his rough manhood and her virginal youth sends sex sparks flying. He has spent 20 days on a raft and 20 years in foreign lands, seven in sexual embrace with the divine Calypso, whereas she has the night before dreamed of marriage. Marriage is a theme of their conversation, and Odysseus believes that the man who possesses Nausicaa will be fortunate indeed:

For nothing is greater or better than this, when a man and a woman keep house together, sharing one heart and mind, a great grief to their foes and a joy to their friends, while their own fame is unsurpassed. (*Od.* 6.182–5)

Marriage is the very institution that the suitors threaten back on Ithaca through their greed and lust. In the *Iliad* the marriage of Hector and Andromache was a tragedy and the marriage of Helen and Paris a farce. The marriage of Odysseus and Nausicaa is an impossibility, no matter how much they desire it. Odysseus is the man who knows that you must defer temporary satisfaction if you want to obtain your deep desires: Odysseus must be careful not to offend Nausicaa's father and mother, the king and queen, without whose help he cannot return home.

The scene is structured like the folktale of the *Frog Prince*, well known from the Grimm collection. A maid drops a ball into a well, which a frog retrieves. When she kisses the frog, it turns into a prince, who marries her. Similarly, one of Nausicaa's girlfriends throws a ball into the stream and wakes Odysseus, a veritable monster to see and to contemplate. However, Odysseus cannot marry Nausicaa, according to the folktale pattern that moves his narrative. Nausicaa, having fulfilled her function of ensuring Odysseus' entrance into the palace, drops from the story, appearing again only briefly.

At a distance, for modesty, Odysseus follows Nausicaa to town, but circumspectly veers off before anyone sees them together. Athena meets him disguised as a little girl (the hero's helper common in folktale) and directs him to the palace. Nausicaa has advised him (and Athena repeats the advice) to throw himself on the mercy of Queen Arete. Concealed by a mist, he enters the throne room, approaches the queen, clasps her knees, and asks for passage home.

No one knows why Odysseus needs to approach Arete instead of the king, who in any event immediately approves the stranger's request for a voyage home. Perhaps the event belongs to the pattern of the female who first is hostile, then friendly to Odysseus' *nostos*. Thus Calypso wanted to hold him back, then helps him prepare his journey to Scheria. Circe (as we will see) wanted to enchant or unman Odysseus, then helped with his further journey. The Phaeacians are not entirely friendly (as will soon be clear); they, like the Cyclopes, are descended from Poseidon. Odysseus' entrance into the palace in disguise, a potential suitor to the princess, is parallel to his disguised penetration of the palace on Ithaca, where he competes with suitors for possession of the lady of the house.

At last Arete asks, "Where did you get those clothes?" rightly suspecting that something is up between Odysseus and her daughter. With considerable delicacy the stranger explains his good intentions, but King Alcinous comes forth and actually offers him Nausicaa's hand!

"Stranger at the Contest" (Book 8)

The Phaeacians live at the edge of magic land – they are living in paradise. As if a divine being had appeared among them, so Odysseus seems to the Phaeacians (thanks to Athena's advocacy). Like the denizens of magic land, they too, in a curious way, are Odysseus' adversaries, according to the folktale pattern that Homer is following, so

> Athena made him taller and sturdier to behold, that he might be welcomed by all the Phaeacians and win awe and reverence, and accomplish the many feats wherein the Phaeacians made trial of Odysseus. (*Od.* 8.20–3)

Before the trials, King Alcinous will hold a fine feast. Nestor hosted Telemachus, Menelaus hosted Telemachus, Calypso hosted Odysseus, and the Phaeacians will host Odysseus, the best feast of all, with Demodocus the famed *aoidos* as entertainer. We cannot help but see in Demodocus Homer's own self-portrait:

> Then the herald drew near, leading the good *aoidos*, whom the Muse loved above all other men, and gave him both good and evil. Of his sight she deprived him, but gave him the gift of sweet song. For him Pontonous, the herald, set a silver-studded chair in the midst of the banqueters, leaning it against a tall pillar, and he hung the clear-toned lyre from a peg close above his head, and showed him how to reach it with his hands. And beside him he placed a basket and a beautiful table, and a cup of wine, to drink when his heart should bid him. (*Od.* 8.62–70)

From this passage seems to descend the legend that Homer was blind, but his extraordinary visual sense makes this unlikely.

Demodocus sings a song about which we know absolutely nothing otherwise, the "Quarrel of Achilles and Odysseus." Presumably he refers obliquely to the *Iliad*, which is also about a quarrel between the captains. Odysseus' tears at the song might have sparked the recognition scene in reply to "Why are you crying?" but Homer wants to stretch out his narrative as long as he can, to enhance the force of this recognition.

They retire to the playing field where, after contests similar to the funeral games for Patroclus in the *Iliad*, a Phaeacian noble taunts Odysseus, saying he could never perform athletics himself, obviously coming from a lower social class. Odysseus rebukes the insult, then proves his aristocratic background by throwing the discus far past all others. He is a real warrior, yes, from the real world, and clearly a social equal to the seafaring Phaeacians. Alcinous apologizes to the stranger and explains the Phaeacian character (which some have suspected of flattering the seafaring Euboeans):

> We are not faultless boxers or wrestlers, but in the foot race we run swiftly, and we are the best seamen, and we love the banquet and the lyre and the dance and changes of garments and warm baths, and the couch. (*Od.* 8.246–9)

To ease the tension, Alcinous summons Demodocus again, who must be an accomplished musician, in addition to his skills at *aoidic* song. He plays for a complex acrobatic dance at which the Phaeacians are adept. Then he sings the notorious "Adultery of Ares and Aphrodite," a song suited to a typical mood of his audience with its theme of sexual betrayal and the near-pornographic image of the naked sex goddess locked in the embrace of the naked god of war while the other male gods get a good look. Homer could never have sung such a song before respectable women, and Demodocus sings before an all-male crowd. The song is a joke whose punch line comes when Apollo nudges Hermes. Would he mind being in Ares' position? Not at all! Hermes says. The song's theme cleverly echoes in jocular form the deadly serious love triangle of Menelaus/Helen/Paris, which caused the Trojan War and led to the death of thousands, including Paris, as it echoes the triangle of Agamemnon/Clytemnestra/Aegisthus, which led to the deaths of Agamemnon, Aegisthus, and Clytemnestra. The love triangle Odysseus/Penelope/suitors will have a different outcome, thanks to a woman who knew how to say "No."

Time still for acrobatics, then to the palace for a bath at the hands of princesses, an endearing custom several times repeated in the *Odyssey*. The glorified Odysseus sees Nausicaa one more time, and she makes a poignant farewell:

> Farewell, stranger, and hereafter even in your own native land may you remember me, for to me first you owe the price of your life. (*Od.* 8.461–2)

She could not marry him, but she did save him, a kind of surrogate mother who received him naked from the sea.

What follows is of extreme interest to literary historians because Homer describes how an *aoidos* functions. Odysseus asks for a song "about the Trojan horse," a theme not a title, and Demodocus "takes up the tale" from the time when the Achaeans have sailed away, as if the "tale" were out there someplace waiting for him. Odysseus is testing the *aoidos* on his knowledge of the tradition:

> If you indeed tell me this tale as it should be told, I will declare to all mankind that the god has with a ready heart granted you the gift of divine *aoidê* [song]. (*Od.* 8.496–8)

Still, Demodocus begins where he wants and goes on as he pleases until, for a second time, Odysseus weeps, setting up the dramatic recognition and midpoint of the plot of the *Odyssey*. Why, he is the very man about whom the song is sung, Odysseus the man of many turns.

First Group: "Cicones, Lotus-eaters, Cyclops" (Book 9)

Odysseus is also the man of many sufferings, enduring one agony after the other. He did it for *kleos* ("fame") and he does it for home:

> I am Odysseus, son of Laertes, known to all men for my stratagems, and my *kleos* rises to heaven. I dwell in clear-seen Ithaca, wherein is a Mount Neritos, covered with waving forests, conspicuous from far away, and round it lie many islands close by one another, Dulichium and Samê and wooded Zacynthus. Ithaca itself lies close in to the mainland the furthest toward the gloom, but the others lie apart toward the dawn and the sun – a rugged island but a good nurse of young men and for myself I can see no other thing sweeter than one's own land. (*Od.* 9.19–28)

No one has explained how Ithaca can be "furthest toward the gloom," because others of the Ionian group lie further westward, and we are not clear what islands he means by Dulichium (Lefkas?), Samê (Cephallenia?), and Zacynthus (?). Still, in other details Homer seems to have firsthand knowledge of the island.

Now begin the most famous adventures in literature, what many think of as being the subject of the *Odyssey*, although the poem is more interested in domestic drama than magical adventure. The adventures are organized into four groups of three, each group consisting of two short adventures and one long adventure, with the journey to the underworld in the center. The adventures begin in a recognizable world, the land of the Cicones, a real tribe in Thrace northwest of Troy, an adventure that duplicates in miniature the assault on Troy. Once again the Achaeans are bandits looting and pillaging a city, but this time events do not go their way. Against the advice of Odysseus, the Ithacans do not depart immediately. On the next day the Cicones overrun them and kill six men from every boat (as six men will die in the cave of Cyclops and six in the tentacles of Scylla). A central theme of Odysseus' *nostos* is the tension between the leader and his men. They give in to greed and hunger, to the belly (like the suitors), while Odysseus remembers (usually) his purpose beyond temporary desire: to get home (to be born again).

Off Cape Malea, the storm-riven southeast tip of the Peloponnesus on the East–West route of Euboean sailors, a storm drives them for nine days and nine nights deep into never-never land. The Lotus-eaters are happy, but drugged. When Odysseus' men eat the lotus, they forget their need to go home. Real lotus plants are not narcotic, although they are a sacred plant in Egyptian religious art. Perhaps we should think of the Lotus-eaters as on the coast of Africa.

The first long story is the adventure of Polyphemus the Cyclops ("round-eye"), one of the best-known folktales in the world. Odysseus' landing on an island opposite Cyclops' land reveals the keen eye of the colonist, and he sees straight away how the land could be developed and improved. Unfortunately, the race of Cyclopes does not know the arts of civilization, of agriculture, and of seafaring. They have no political life, but live in single-family units. They don't make bread. They are powerful but stupid and on a realistic level represent the foreign peoples with whom Greek colonists contended in western lands.

Above all, Polyphemus does not respect the rules of *xenia*, as shown to Telemachus at Pylos and Sparta. Odysseus spends days on Scheria before anyone asks who he is, whereas Polyphemus, when first seeing the scrawny Greeks, immediately asks "Who are you?" Instead of feeding his guests, he eats them! As gift-token to Odysseus, he will eat him last. Polyphemus is like the suitors who devour Odysseus' substance, but in the end are destroyed by a trick, when a man pretending to be somebody else enters the dark hall of feasting.

Odysseus' trick is to tell Polyphemus that his name is Nobody, as he is locked inside the cave, even as death ruins identity. Like many heroes in folktale, Odysseus makes the death monster drunk, overcomes him by a trick, and maims him with a special weapon (the sharpened stake).

When he is reborn into the light, he declares his name. "I am Odysseus!" he shouts and, yes, long before, Polyphemus received a prophecy that a certain Odysseus would do him harm. As Odysseus and his men row away, the Cyclops invites him back to the cave, where he can show him proper *xenia* and give him gift-tokens aplenty.

Polyphemus, like all the Cyclopes, is the offspring of Poseidon, god of the sea. When blinded, he calls on his father to curse Odysseus with years of wandering and a harsh return. Poseidon is god of the sea, and the sea is Odysseus' enemy, representing dissolution, death, and chaos. The curse of Polyphemus is a mythical explanation of why Odysseus suffers, a persecution that stands in curious contrast to Zeus' moralizing about human beings causing their own problems. Of course, Odysseus *did* blind Polyphemus, but who can blame him for that?

Second Group: "Aeolus, Laestrygonians, Circe" (Book 10)

Odysseus has had to deal with Cicones, ordinary men; drugs in Lotus Land; a cannibal giant; and now with a lord of the elements, King Aeolus, who lives as a god at perpetual feast, where dine his 12 sons and daughters, married to one another in incestuous union.[11] The story is pure folktale. The Wind King gave the hero a boon – all the bad winds in a bag and only the good left to blow – with the prohibition common in folktales: Don't open that bag! The treacherous followers, suspecting their leader of the gluttony that eats at their own insides, do so anyway and pay the price. The story is a natural for Homer's theme of crime and punishment, and we see how far we have come from a realistic mode of narrative when Odysseus sails for a magical nine days and nine nights and only when he is so close to shore that he can "see smoke" does he fall asleep. His men's greed and his own inclination to sleep are the enemy. Any man with so much against him must be the dangerous object of superhuman anger, as Aeolus emphasizes when expelling the disobedient traveler who returns. For Odysseus to survive, he must wake (from the sleep of death).

The land of the Laestrygonians looks so northern, it seems to testify to a common European store of folktales. Odysseus' men come to a narrow harbor, rather like a fjord, but without explanation he alone moors his ship outside. There seem to be 12 ships (as stated in the "Catalogue of Ships" at *Iliad* 2.637), so the other 11 ships go inside. A party goes inland and meets a girl at a well, a folktale motif. The

Laestrygonians rush forth and spear the helpless Achaeans – like shooting fish in a barrel: they are monstrous cannibal giants and doublets of the Cyclopes. Only Odysseus escapes, through the trick of having moored outside the fjord. He must have known in advance that something was up, used his *mêtis* ("mind") to foresee danger, and taken evasive action. One of Odysseus' epithets is *polymêtis*: "with many minds."

The *Odyssey* is surely much concerned with relationships between the sexes and with the power that each sex holds over the other. In the symphony of female types in the *Odyssey*, Circe in the long adventure in the second group is the preeminent seductress. She stands just before his descent to the underworld, then receives him from the underworld when he returns. She is death as woman and seductress, then becomes life and prophecy and hope according to the strange ambiguity of the *Odyssey*'s females.

The flavor of this story, too, has reminded many commentators of folktales from northern lands. Odysseus at first kills a stag, in folktale a motif precedent to the meeting with a sorcerer or witch. Circe lives in the middle of a deep dark forest, smoke trailing into the sky. Follow that smoke, and you will find the witch. On the other hand, as the daughter of Helius and the brother of Aeetes, king of Colchis at the eastern end of the Black Sea where Jason traveled to get the Golden Fleece, Circe belongs in the East, and some have thought that the incident is modified from one in the *Argonautica*. Still, from a very early time speculation placed Circe's island somewhere in the Bay of Naples (there is still a Monte Circeo near Sorrento). Homer says that you cannot see where the sun rises or sets; that is, the island lies somewhere over there, through the looking glass. But when they leave, and Odysseus begins the second set of six stories, the sun rises over the island.

To know Circe is to become a pig. Like the Lotus-eaters, she laces her food with drugs that prevent your homegoing. She is beautiful, the female force that reduces the male to a disgusting snorting animal, fond of eating excrement, a comic pose effective still in entertainment today. She means to harm Odysseus: if she cannot change him into an animal, she will remove his testicles, according to the prediction of Hermes, who appears to the hero in the dark wood and gives him *moly*, a potent talisman. This is the only time in the adventures that a god appears directly to Odysseus, and again it is not Athena, whose *mêtis* belongs to the upper world, but the magician Hermes, who joins this world with the next.

Hermes instructs Odysseus how to behave. He must tame this woman (who is death). He must place her under his power by holding a weapon at her throat and forcing her to forswear harm. Then she will be his.

When overcome, Circe recognizes Odysseus. Hermes, who saved Odysseus, had prophesied long before that a certain Odysseus would overcome her, she said. Once she has sworn to do him no harm, and they have gone to bed, Circe becomes the ideal hostess. Like Siduri, the "divine ale-maid" who meets Gilgamesh at the edge of the waters at the edge of the world, Circe sends Odysseus on his most dangerous exploit: a journey to the land of the dead. When you return from there, surely you are born again.

"Land of the Dead" (Book 11)

In general the "songs" of the *Odyssey* follow the folktale pattern of arrival/conflict/recognition/resolution, but the "Land of the Dead" is instead a succession of catalogues. This unit must owe its building blocks to the genre of catalogue poetry (which influences Hesiod, Homer's contemporary, so much). Following Circe's instructions, Odysseus travels across the river Ocean, usually thought to flow around the world in a gigantic circle, to the "land of the Cimmerians." The Cimmerians were a historical people who lived north of the Black Sea, here mythologized into denizens of another world.

At first Odysseus doesn't appear to be in the underworld, the House of Hades, because in order to communicate with the dead he behaves as a necromancer, a black magician. He kills black rams over a pit. In an uncanny scene the *psychai* ("breath-souls") gather around the blood, which in death they have lost, so that for a moment they may return to consciousness: "the life is in the blood," as in the biblical saying. Odysseus holds them back with his sword, which has become a magician's wand through which he controls the insubstantial spirits.

Elpenor is first to speak. He does not drink the blood because his *psychê* is not yet "laid," ritually banished from this world to the next, thus remaining a danger to others and a torment to himself. He begs for proper burial. Teiresias comes next and drinks. Teiresias tells Odysseus of trouble at home and his certain victory. One day he must go far inland to where they have never heard of the sea and sacrifice to Poseidon, god of the sea. Only by extending Poseidon's power, whose son he has blinded, can Odysseus placate his enemy the sea, which is death, which stands between Odysseus and home. In the end, Teiresias says, he will die a "gentle death from the sea" (11.134–5). The prophecy was taken in the later, rationalizing, tradition to refer to a spear point made from a stingray wielded by Telegonus, Odysseus' son by Circe, who accidentally kills his father (the *Odyssey* divulges nothing about a son by Circe). Death is death and no one escapes it, but Odysseus' death will be gentle, unlike the deaths of Hector, Priam, Achilles, Patroclus, Agamemnon, and Ajax. Such is the reward of the wily man.

Odysseus speaks with his mother, who died pathetically longing for him. Although Teiresias mentions the suitors, Odysseus' mother knows only about a time ten years before Odysseus returns home, when Telemachus was still "unharassed" in the house; she has no prophetic power. Then comes a "Catalogue of Famous Women," including Alcmene, mother of Heracles, and Leda, mother of Helen of Troy and of Clytemnestra, and Ariadne, wife of Theseus, and many others, some quite obscure in the later canon of Greek myth.

The catalogue of women caps the first group of three interviews and is a good time for intermission. The Phaeacians are astounded at Odysseus' power to tell a tale. Truly he has behaved as an exemplary *aoidos* (although he does not use a lyre), holding his audience spellbound at a banquet. Although Odysseus says he would like to get some rest, they will not let him, wanting more.

In the second group of three *psychai* Homer returns to the paradigm of Agamemnon and Clytemnestra. Up comes the *psychê* of Agamemnon. He tells how he and his companions died, murdered at a banquet (just as Odysseus will kill the suitors at a banquet). He curses the race of women (the dead suitors think that Penelope was behind it all) and praises Odysseus for his good fortune in having a wife like Penelope. Uh, on second thought:

> And another thing will I tell you, and do you lay it to heart: in secret and not openly bring your ship to the shore of your dear native land, for you can never trust a woman. (*Od*. 11.454–6)

You have to be careful even with Penelope – a rare flash of humor in this poem.

Now the *psychê* of Achilles appears. Odysseus comforts him with his *kleos* in the memory of the world, but Achilles makes a famous reply:

> No, seek not to speak soothingly to me of death, glorious Odysseus. I would choose, if I might live on earth, to serve as the hireling of another, of some man without a portion, whose livelihood was small, rather than be lord over all the dead that have perished. (*Od*. 11.488–91)

So dear to the Greek was this world and the things in it, and so gloomy the world to come. Achilles, like Odysseus, wants to know about his son, Neoptolemus.

The third *psychê* of this group to approach the blood is Ajax, son of Telamon, who killed himself after going mad. He does not drink, for he will not speak to Odysseus, who was awarded the dead Achilles' arms when Ajax deserved them, as everyone knows.

Homer seems to forget that Odysseus is interrogating ghosts at the side of a pit of blood and now launches into a "Catalogue of Sinners." Odysseus seems to be in the underworld itself as Homer describes the celebrated punishments of Tityus, Tantalus, and Sisyphus. He sees Heracles, but it is only a phantom, an *eidolon* ("image"). The real Heracles is in Heaven, married to Hêbê ("youth"). Suddenly, a swarm of *psychai* frightens Odysseus. He fears that the Gorgon's head may appear. He breaks off the necromancy and returns to his ship.

"Sirens," "Scylla and Charybdis," and "Cattle of Helius" (Book 12)

Ostensibly Odysseus crossed the river Ocean to learn from Teiresias how he might arrive home. Teiresias did not tell him, but when Odysseus returns to Circe's island, she gives precise instructions about the dangers that lie ahead and what he must do. The last three stories of Odysseus' adventures are so well known that it is hard to read them as an integral part of the poem; we do wonder how they must have sounded to a Greek audience.

The Sirens (whence our "siren") represent, like Circe, the deadly female force: alluring, irresistible, but death dealing. They embody a curious exaggeration of the power of the *aoidos*, whose song "delights," as Homer says several times; their song also delights, but the price is death. The story has elements in common with the biblical folktale of Adam and Eve, who ate from the Tree of the Knowledge of Good and Evil, because the Sirens, too, offer knowledge:

> Come here, as you travel, renowned Odysseus, great glory of the Achaeans. Stay your ship that you may listen to the voice of us two. For never yet has any man rowed past this island in his black ship until he has heard the sweet voice from our lips. No, he has joy of it and goes his way a wiser man. For we know all the toils that in wide Troy the Argives and Trojans endured through the will of the gods, and we know all things that come to pass upon the fruitful earth. (*Od.* 12.184–91)

The Sirens, like Homer, know all about what happened at Troy and can answer any questions you might have. Adam and Eve were expelled from the garden for eating the fruit of the tree, but Odysseus through his *mêtis* has his cake and eats it. He foresees that he will cry out for release, but tricks his own will by ordering his men to invert the meaning of his words and tie him tighter. In this story, as in the adventures generally, Odysseus is not so much a character in literature as a symbol for the human spirit, lusting for delicious and sensual adventure without having to pay the awful price. Intelligence is the trick that makes this possible.

Because Circe has set forth precise instructions, we can admire Odysseus' remaining silent to his men about Scylla and Charybdis. Scylla, too, is female, but wholly a monster, with six heads and twelve snaky legs and barking like a dog, a demon of death. Circe has warned him that Charybdis is death for all, but that Scylla, against whom no defense is possible, will take six (as died per boat at Ismarus, as died in the cave of Cyclops). Still, Odysseus arms himself, a warrior to the end in brazen defiance of Circe's advice. It does him no good.

The long adventure in this third triad of adventures is on Thrinacria, the island of Helius, the sun. From an early time Thrinacria was thought to be Sicily, as Scylla and Charybdis appear to be a mythicization of the perilous Straits of Messina between the toe of the boot of Italy and the island of Sicily. Euboean sailors traveled through these very waters in the early eighth century BC, and still today Italian tourism promotes Sicily as the "island of the sun."

This folktale, too, turns on the violated prohibition, but one wonders how Helius has come into the story, a god who almost never appears in Greek myth except as a witness to oaths. A curious Egyptian story called the "Shipwrecked Sailor" survives from the second millennium BC, in which a sailor lands on the Island of Ra, the sun god, and the motif may somehow descend to Homer from this source (but in the Egyptian story only a kindly snake lives on the island). The 350 cattle of Helius seem to stand for the roughly 350 days of the year.

As we have seen, Homer singles out this story in the poem's prologue to encapsulate all of the adventures, and it contains central motifs. Odysseus falls asleep in the hills while his men eat cattle, as he fell asleep just off the shores of Ithaca when coming from the island of Aeolus. Again his men are restive and obey the call of the belly over their purpose – to bring themselves home alive.

And so they died, all but one, as often in folktale. And now he is alone.

"Return of Odysseus" (Book 13)

The hero must bring back treasures from his journey, and the Phaeacians more than make up for all the lost booty Odysseus carried from Troy. They provide magical transport, linking the dark world of the high seas and its symbols of death to the bright world of home and its affirmation of life. Repeatedly, sleep or narcosis threatened Odysseus, and now again he falls asleep:

> Then for Odysseus they spread a rug and a linen sheet on the deck of the hollow ship at the stern, that he might sleep soundly, and he too went aboard, and lay down in silence. Then they sat down on the benches, each in order, and let loose the hawser from the pierced stone. And as soon as they leaned back and tossed the brine with their oar blades, sweet sleep fell upon his eyes, an unawakening sleep, most sweet, and most like to death. (*Od.* 13.73–80)

The Phaeacians deposit him on the shore asleep near an olive tree and a cave of the nymphs and place his treasures beside them. It is dawn, a new day and a new birth. The olive tree is life (Odysseus hung from a tree over Charybdis and, as we learn, his wedding bed is built into a tree). Poseidon, grudging the Phaeacians their role as transporters of forlorn men, turns their ship into stone, taken according to later explanation to be a large rock in the harbor of Corcyra (which Thucydides says is Phaeacia). No more will they bind the two worlds with their fairy magic. The Phaeacians were meant for Odysseus alone, and what applied to him does not apply to you and me. The petrifaction of the Phaeacian ship is a symbol for the end of the heroic age. Now things are different and there is no going back.

Homer displays detailed knowledge of Ithacan geography when he describes the harbor of Phorcys as bounded by two steep headlands and just off it a cave of the nymphs, a good description of the modern harbor of Vathy, "deep," on the east shore of Ithaca. Ithaca is a small hourglass-shaped island running north–south, one of the so-called Ionian group west of the entrance to the Gulf of Corinth. Ithaca has a second good harbor on the other side and other end of the island, on the western tip that faces modern Cephallenia, which Homer seems to call Samê, the modern name of the harbor village on Cephallenia that faces Ithaca.

There really is a cave up from the harbor of Vathy with two openings, as Homer says of the cave of the nymphs. In another cave near the other harbor (near modern Stavros) were found pieces of 13 bronze tripods, which seem to have been set up in the late ninth century BC. Inscriptions from the third century BC prove that the cave was then a shrine to Odysseus, but we cannot be sure how early the identification was made. There are no parallels for this archeological find. Some have speculated that Homer must have known about these tripods when he says that Odysseus returned with "tough bronze" (13.368) that he put in a cave, or the poem may even have existed as a text already by then and inspired the dedication of tripods.

Arriving in the land of the Laestrygonians, Odysseus' crew met up with the king's daughter; in Scheria, Odysseus met Nausicaa; and now he meets Athena disguised as a youth. Only Odysseus and Athena appear in disguise in the poem. Here begins an opera of lying tales, nearly a subgenre within the *Odyssey*, so much of which is made up of tales: those that Nestor tells, and Menelaus tells, and Odysseus tells in the land of the Phaeacians. Tales, more tales, and the narrative is little advanced. These lying tales follow patterns close to those of the "true" tales that Odysseus told to the Phaeacians, but instead they are set in the post-heroic realistic world with its everyday acts of treachery, murder, piracy, and trade.

In the first recognition scene on Ithaca Odysseus deceptively describes to Athena, who embodies worldly *mêtis*, how he hailed from Crete. He is a Trojan fighter, but also a murderer and an outcast whom the Phoenicians have deposited asleep on the island. The Phoenicians are like the Phaeacians (the names are similar), but in Homer's topsy-turvy fictional world the magical Phaeacians are "real" whereas the historical Phoenicians have become "fictional"!

Some think that this story, and the ones to come that connect Odysseus to Crete, may reflect other, earlier, or alternate versions of the *Odyssey*, a view supported by two extra lines that appear in Book 1 in some manuscripts. Athena describes Telemachus' journey to Pylos and Sparta "and from there to Crete to King Idomeneus, who came home second of the bronze-clad Achaeans." This plausible explanation suggests that other *Odyssey*s were not so engaged in otherworldly symbolic travel (such criticism is called neo-analysis). Homer had extra material about crete and, because he has all the time in the world, he puts it in.

Odysseus' love of a good story that is untrue, which through cleverness attempts to disguise and disarm, endears Athena to him. They are like lovers who have not seen each other for a long time. Odysseus mentions that he has not seen her since he was lost at sea, a detail of which Homer is therefore conscious. Athena helps him hide the treasure, never mentioned again. She predicts death for the murderous and ravenous suitors.

"Odysseus and the Swineherd" (Book 14)

After much aristocratic entertainment, Odysseus now sojourns with the humble swineherd Eumaeus, whom Homer speaks to directly and affectionately as "O my swineherd." Eumaeus is the moral and structural equal to the Phaeacians and the direct opposite of the Cyclops. Circe, too, was a swineherd. Golden dogs stood before the house of Alcinous, as here savage dogs run at Odysseus and nearly kill him. Homer describes with penetrating realism Eumaeus' house and the sties that he built, using the kind of language common in the *Iliad* in the similes.

Eumaeus has little – thanks to the rapacity of the suitors! – but freely he offers hospitality to his guest according to the fair prescriptions of *xenia*. Odysseus needs a cloak to cover his rags. He "predicts" that Odysseus will arrive that very day. In return for his prediction, he expects Eumaeus to give him a cloak, which, Odysseus says, he will not take if his prediction is untrue. The scene is deeply ironical, because of course Odysseus even then sits before Eumaeus. A cloak from Eumaeus is like gold from the Phaeacians. We already felt the irony that comes from disguise when Odysseus moved unrecognized among the Phaeacians, and the theme pervades the rest of the poem, or is its central motif.

To prove that Odysseus is near (so Eumaeus better get ready to surrender the cloak), Odysseus tells a second Cretan tale, a reformation of the story we heard at the banquet of the Phaeacians. As then he attacked the Cicones in Thrace, now he attacks Egypt, with the same disastrous results. As the Phaeacians gave him treasure, so does he amass treasure in Egypt. As the Phaeacians brought him to Ithaca, now the Phoenicians carry him there, meaning to sell him as a slave. But their boat was struck by lightning, as happened to Odysseus and his men when they left the island of the Cattle of the Sun. As then he rode a keel, now he rides a mast, landing in Thresprotia on the mainland across from Ithaca. In Thresprotia, Odysseus claims, he left his treasure and went up to the oracle of Dodona, even as Odysseus sought news of his homecoming from Teiresias. Odysseus thought that the Phaeacians had betrayed him when he first awoke on Ithaca, and now the Thresprotians, commissioned to convey the Cretan Odysseus to Dulichium, betray him and plan to sell him as a slave. He narrowly escapes.

Eumaeus still does not believe the stranger's prediction that the master will soon return, in which case he would be obligated to give the stranger a cloak. Odysseus tells a parable about how once at Troy none other than Odysseus got a cloak for him by a trick. Even now Odysseus is trying to get a cloak for the stranger/Odysseus through the trick of pretending to be somebody else! The friendly Eumaeus accepts the moral of the tale and agrees that the beggar should have a cloak, but alas he has no extra. When Telemachus returns, then he can get his cloak. And so the slave entertains the master and in his gracious hospitality casts into strong relief the immoral audacity of the free aristocracy who pummel modesty and besiege Odysseus' house.

"Return of Telemachus" (15.1–300; 493–557) and "Story of Eumaeus the Slave" (15.301–492)

Meanwhile, back in Sparta, puppet-master Athena informs Telemachus of his danger from the suitors' ambush and warns him that his mother is about to marry one of them and take what belongs to him. Penelope in the parallel schemes of Penelope/Odysseus/Telemachus and Clytemnestra/Agamemnon/Orestes is the good and faithful wife, but there are repeated hints of her weakness and the great danger she may offer to the recreation of order; already the ghost of Agamemnon has warned Odysseus about coming home openly, lest he fall into a trap of Penelope's devising.

As Telemachus is about to embark, the strange prophet Theoclymenus appears, a descendant of Melampus, who founded a family of eminent prophets. We hear about the ancestors of Theoclymenus in an interesting digression, but why does Homer suddenly introduce a new character? Some have thought that in another version of the poem "Theoclymenus" was Odysseus in disguise. His only function is later to prophesy doom to the suitors, but this function is critical: both Polyphemus and Circe received prophesies that Odysseus would overcome them, and so too the suitors must learn from a prophecy of their impending doom. The episode also draws attention to the new-won maturity of Telemachus, who went abroad to become a man. As a homicide, Theoclymenus is dangerous, but Telemachus' new authority does not hesitate to bring him on board.

Meanwhile, back on Ithaca, Eumaeus tells a remarkable story of his own. Like Odysseus, he is a prince, his father a king of an island called Syriê, a place renowned (as is Phaeacia) for its peace and wealth, remotely placed, north of Ortygia, Calypso's island. Phoenicians are treacherous, that's for sure, and so are women, and most treacherous is a Phoenician woman. One served in the palace of the king of Syriê, but when seduced by a Phoenician trader, she stole the prince, along with valuable cups from the table. Eumaeus is like Odysseus in being a prince reduced to low social status, but the story is like that of Paris and Helen. Helen, too, betrayed her household, stole the dinnerware, and ran away with her lover, bringing unhappiness to all.

"Recognition of Odysseus and Telemachus" (Book 16)

While Odysseus is in quest of home, Telemachus is in quest of his father, from whom he has been separated for a long time. The son searching for the father is a theme of deep resonance. Jesus used it to illustrate the relationship between God and man. The meeting of father and son is therefore plot point two, from which the rest of the story flows: the just revenge exacted upon the suitors and the reestablishment of order in the house and in the kingdom.

At Athena's prompting, Telemachus makes his way to Eumaeus' hut. With enormous irony his own father, whom he has traveled so far to find, sits before him, unrecognized. When Odysseus hears again of the situation at the house, he says, "I wish I were Odysseus":

> Would that with my present temper I were as young as you, either the son of blameless Odysseus, or Odysseus himself; then might some stranger cut off my head from my neck, if I did not prove myself the curse of them all when I had come to the halls of Odysseus, son of Laertes. (*Od.* 16.99–104)

After Telemachus sends Eumaeus to the house to report to Penelope that he has safely returned, Athena summons Odysseus from the hut and as in a fairytale strikes him with her wand, transforming him. Inhuman forces are at work, and not for the first time. Telemachus at first takes his transformed father for a god and cannot believe that he is his father, returned as it were from the dead. Miracles won't do, Odysseus must persuade him! A natural logician, Odysseus adduces the fact of his transformation as proof that he is Odysseus. We expect some kind of token in a recognition scene, something tangible that proves identity, but here Odysseus' familiarity with Athena will have to satisfy.

At last Telemachus gives in, the first of two climactic recognition scenes on Ithaca, the second being with Penelope. Telemachus wants to be like his father and now they are arm in arm, wetting the floor with tears, plotting death to their enemies. Homer deftly pulls together the strands of two plots, the return of the son and the return of the father. Because the boat that carried Telemachus has now landed in the harbor, the suitors realize that their own murderous plot is foiled. From the boat a messenger goes to tell Penelope that Telemachus is safe and meets Eumaeus bent on the same errand.

In the meantime, Odysseus instructs Telemachus in a trick to remove all the armor from the walls except for two shields and two spears, which they can take hold of and use against the suitors. Later, Homer forgets all about this plan when Eumaeus and Philoetius, the swineherd and cowherd, join the plot. According to Telemachus' earlier report, there are 108 suitors, plus an *aoidos* (who sings against his will) and a herald and ten retainers: a total of 120 men. Even if they are armed, their chances are slim against so many.

Early in the poem Penelope ventured into the den of the suitors to protest against Phemius' song about the Trojan War, and now she again shows herself in obnoxious company. She complains about their desire to harm her son and reminds them how Odysseus had helped their families, but the lying Eurymachus denies everything.

Eumaeus returns to the hut. The fairy godmother Athena has made Odysseus again miserable to look upon. With such backing, one wonders how they can lose.

"Beggar in his Own House" (Book 17)

Odysseus is at the bottom of the social ladder, the scum of the earth. In the land of the Laestrygonians, when he went inland, he met the evil king's daughter at a well; here at a well he meets another bad guy, Melantheus ("blackie"). Blackie kicks his master in the rear and insults him and threatens his son. Could Achilles have withstood the urge to disembowel the pipsqueak on the spot? Odysseus sees his purpose and swallows his wrath.

Polyphemus recognized Odysseus when he shouted out his name; Circe recognized him when he defied her magic. In the symbolic language of the adventures the recognition is a kind of new birth, a transcendence over the enemies of narcosis, sleep, and death. On Ithaca recognition serves more closely the dramatic structure. Odysseus is not what he seems to be – he is in disguise. Through his *métis* (and Athena's help) he is invisible and can see what others cannot see. He is going to destroy his enemies, and he is going to do it by a trick.

Piece by piece Odysseus resumes his former identity. When poor Argus ("swifty"), once Odysseus' favorite sporting dog, recognizes his master at the door, Odysseus again becomes master of the hounds. Argus' recognition is also proof that his disguise can be penetrated, and is emblematic of the decay fallen on the house since Odysseus left. The dog's pathetic death on a dunghill outside the door to the court makes us wonder about the wealth of real kings in Homer's day. Argus corresponds to the golden dogs before the house of Alcinous, the dogs outside Eumaeus' hut, and even the barking dogs of Scylla. In myth the dog Cerberus stood before the gates of Hades' house.

We cannot reconstruct Odysseus' house very well from Homer's descriptions, but it is a simple structure. In front is a courtyard. A door leads off the court into a large hall, in the center of which is a hearth. The roof must be open in the center of the hall to allow smoke to escape. The floor is packed earth. There are pillars in this hearth room supporting the roof. Upstairs are the women's quarters and a storeroom, perhaps off a hall.

Everywhere are signs that something is up, but Penelope stubbornly refuses to see, or pretends not to. Homer doesn't tell us Penelope's inmost thoughts, and her sometimes mysterious behavior inspires speculation. Telemachus has told his mother about Menelaus' report that Odysseus was trapped on an island. Theoclymenus, the mysterious prophet, declares that even then Odysseus is on the island. Yet neither prophecy impresses Penelope.

The "beggar" crouches at the back of the hearth room against a pillar. When the arrogant bully Antinous complains, Eumaeus provides interesting information about the life of an *aoidos*:

> Antinous, you speak not well, noble though you are. Who by himself ever seeks out and invites a stranger from abroad, unless it is one of those who

are masters of a public craft, a prophet, or a healer of sickness, or a builder, yes, or a divine *aoidos*, who gives delight with his song? For these men are welcomed over all the boundless earth. (*Od.* 17.381–6)

Singers, *aoidoi*, are traveling men it seems, and people accommodate them.

While the master begs in his own house, the suitors consume his food, then are stingy about sharing it. Antinous whacks Odysseus with a footstool. Such men deserve to die. Odysseus tells a cautionary tale about how once he was great, yet fell into ruin (as the suitors might too).

When Penelope hears of how the suitors outrage *xenia* and insult the beggar – after all, the beggar could be a god in disguise – she declares that she wishes to speak to him, a scene we anxiously await, when husband and wife will be brought face to face after 20 years. Will they now recognize one another and the poem come to an end? You would be out of sympathy with Homer's way of telling a story if you thought that could happen.

"Odysseus and the Beggar Iros" (18.1–157) and "Tempting of the Suitors" (18.158–428)

In the atmosphere of disguise, prophecy, and abuse a real beggar suddenly appears, who challenges Odysseus' right to share the threshold. In a boisterous scene of bear-baiting and mock heroic warfare, Odysseus girds up his cloak. Suddenly he doesn't seem so helpless. Throughout this sequence the suitors become ever more nervous about this puzzling stranger. Antinous threatens the real beggar with disembowelment if he should lose the match, a faux "games" scene like the athletic events at the funeral games of Achilles. Odysseus brings Iros down with one fell blow, and "the lordly suitors raised their hands, and nearly died of laughter" (18.99–100). Such hysteria presages death.

We have not seen that much of Penelope in the poem, but from here on she becomes prominent. Suddenly she wishes to present herself before the suitors, but in order to restore her beauty after so much sorrow, she falls asleep (like Odysseus at crucial junctures), and Athena gives her a beauty treatment. Awakened and now radiant (like Odysseus after his transformations), accompanied by two maids and veiled for modesty, she appears on the stairs:

Right away then the knees of the suitors were loosened and their hearts inflamed with sexual desire, and they all prayed, each that he might lie beside her. (*Od.* 18.212–13)

In coy fashion, Penelope pretends concern for the strangers' welfare, but Eurymachus takes the bait and aches for her with slurping words and gaze. Penelope uses their admiration to extort gifts, complaining how in courtship the grooms bring gifts, but all the suitors do is take, take, take. In his mind Odysseus wholly approves of Penelope's clever ploy, and does not object to his wife's use of her sexuality for material gain. Such gain is good, and is as much admired by the wife as it is by the far-traveled husband, and it is threatened fundamentally by the suitors' depredations.

Night falls – time for Odysseus and Penelope to meet. The suitors have set up torches. They drink and dance and the maids prepare to serve their sexual desires; in this way classical symposia, too, would end. The beggar offers to care for the fires, but Melantho, evidently a sister of Melantheus, insults him. Penelope cherished Melantho, but she is Eurymachus' whore, who longs for night and the sex that comes with it. Odysseus dampens her enthusiasm when he explains how Telemachus will have to cut her limb from limb.

Eurymachus, feeling a trace of decency, offers Odysseus a job on his farm, then takes it back, leading to Odysseus' lecture on the kind of farming that is correct for a proper man. Eurymachus thinks this beggar a mad fool or a drunk, and tries to hit him with a stool. The beggar is getting on everyone's nerves.

"Odysseus and Penelope" (19.1–360; 508–604) and "The Scar of Odysseus" (19.361–507)

Once the suitors have gone, Odysseus instructs Telemachus to remove all the armor from the walls and hide it (forgetting his earlier instruction to leave two sets). He can explain how the armor was begrimed by all the smoke in the room; in fact the suitors never notice the missing armor. Because Odysseus has sent the maids to their rooms, Athena herself holds a golden lamp to lead Telemachus to the storeroom (we're not sure where that is), the only reference to a lamp in the Homeric poems. In Homer, torches usually light the way, and lamps are not found in the archeological record until the seventh century BC. Perhaps Athena's lamp is a reminiscence of Bronze Age practice (when lamps were common and part of ritual) if, as many believe, Athena descends from a Minoan goddess.

Penelope comes to sit before the fire. The stranger tells her that Odysseus will soon be home. He claims, again, to be from Crete, and Homer gives us our earliest example of historical geography (except for the *Iliad*'s "Catalogue of Ships"):

> There is a land called Crete in the midst of the wine-dark sea, a fair, rich land, surrounded by water, and on it are many men, past counting, and ninety cities. They have not all the same speech, but their tongues are mixed. There dwell Achaeans, there great-hearted native Cretans, there Cydonians and Dorians of waving plumes and good Pelasgians. (*Od.* 19.172–7)

There is a contemporary ring to Odysseus' Cretan tales, as if Homer were describing conditions he knew first hand. The Achaeans would be the Mycenaeans, the native Cretans no doubt the Minoans, the Cydonians from somewhere, and the Dorians the people from northwest Greece who in classical times dominated the island. This is the only explicit reference to Dorians in the Homeric poems.

The meeting of Odysseus and Penelope alone in the pitch-blackened hall is structured as a recognition scene, which it might have been. Odysseus even elaborately describes a token, a brooch that Odysseus wore when he came to Crete. But it is still too early for the recognition. Some think that in other versions of the poem a recognition did take place at this moment and that husband and wife together planned the slaughter of the suitors. In our *Odyssey*, however, Homer presents a Penelope who doesn't want to believe. She cannot credit his report any more than she believed Telemachus or Theoclymenus, because she has been disappointed so often. She must believe the worst. She thanks the stranger for his tale, then rewards him with a footbath, a courtesy shown to distinguished visitors, not to beggars.

Odysseus agrees to the bath, but will have none of the whorish maids touch his flesh. As if looking for trouble, he asks instead for the one woman in the house who can identify him, as Eurycleia does when she touches the scar on his leg, a recognition token. In the long digression about how Odysseus acquired this scar (one of the longest digressions in Homer) we learn that his grandfather Autolycus ("wolfman") named

him. Homer occasionally plays with words and here Autolycus puns on
Odysseus' name:

> My daughter's husband and my daughter, give him whatever name I say.
> Lo, because as I have come here as "one angered with many" [*odussamenos*],
> both with men and women over the fruitful earth, therefore let the name
> by which the child is named be Odysseus [*odusseus*]. (*Od.* 19.406–9)

The Greek *odussamenos* is of uncertain meaning; it may also mean "he
who has suffered much."

Because Eurycleia nursed Odysseus, she is in a sense his mother, and
this recognition carries him closer to the center of power. He is now
master of the servants. He is hardly sentimental about Eurycleia and
takes her by the throat and threatens violence if she makes a sound.
What else could he do?

The unbelieving, provocative, distracted, and somewhat distant
Penelope doesn't notice a thing as Eurycleia drops the big bronze bowl,
which clangs on the floor. When Odysseus again comes to her side, she
gives another sure prophecy of her husband's return: the dream about
the geese slaughtered by an eagle:

> But come now, hear this dream of mine, and interpret it for me. Twenty
> geese I have in the house that come forth from the water and eat wheat,
> and my heart warms with joy as I watch them. But forth from the moun-
> tain there came a great eagle with crooked beak and broke all their necks
> and killed them and they lay strewn in a heap in the halls, while he was
> borne aloft to the bright sky. Now for my part I wept and wailed, in a
> dream though it was, and around me thronged the fair-tressed Achaean
> women as I grieved piteously because the eagle had slain my geese. (*Od.*
> 19.535–43)

It's easy to see that Penelope regrets the loss of her admirers. There are
numerous omens and portents in the last books of the *Odyssey* to intensify the narrative and emphasize the suitors' dull inability to resist fate,
but one wonders why Homer included this dream. You mean she's
going to miss the suitors?

The inscrutability of Homer's attitude toward his story is deepened by
Penelope's sudden announcement that on the next day she will hold an
archery contest. She will marry whoever wins. What are her motives?
Does she suspect that the stranger is Odysseus? Two thousand years of

commentary have not provided an answer. Of course, Homer needs to bring his song to a conclusion. To do so he needs the archery contest, an occasion for a critical recognition, but without a persuasive psychological motivation. The next day is a feast day for Apollo held at the dark of the moon. Penelope has prayed to Apollo that he kill Antinous (17.494). The object of the contest will be to string a bow, Apollo's weapon, and perform a feat at which Odysseus himself was adept. It looks like a setup, but Homer has sacrificed the logic of his story to his desire to portray Penelope's character as despairing and willful.

"Prophecy of Doom" (Book 20)

In a sexually charged scene, Odysseus lies in the great court, wondering whether to murder the maids who giggle as they go to whore with the suitors, or to wait and kill them later. He should be cheerful, however, because Athena appears to him, a goddess in the house, and promises the support he needs. As Odysseus sleeps, Penelope, just upstairs, awakes, having dreamed that her husband lay beside her, as he nearly does. Gloom, self-pity, and deviousness are all parts of Penelope's character, and in her desire to die she tells a curious story about the daughters of Pandareos, otherwise unknown, as earlier she had told another unknown story about Nightingale, also a daughter of Pandareos.

Odysseus awakes as dawn breaks on another day of infamy. Athena's epiphany was insufficient for a good mood; he prays for omens and gets them. Telemachus goes to town while the faithful Eumaeus, the nasty Melantheus, and a new character, Philoetius the cowherd, who loved Odysseus as no other, bring animals into the court to slaughter for the feast day in honor of Apollo. The court is a slaughter yard where animals are killed and disemboweled; soon it will reek of human blood. Slaughter is on everyone's mind, and the suitors are still thinking about murder when they see that the omens are bad. They decide to get drunk instead.

Just inside, across the threshold, the rowdies cook meat and swill it down with wine. There are many mouths to feed and, like the bloody mouth of the Cyclops, the suitors together comprise a ravenous maw. We wonder whether they really ate ox-hooves, but one is in the basket for a nasty wooer to hurl at the man who owns this house. Somehow Telemachus gets back from town, and Homer gives a taste of the horror to come as Telemachus reproves the suitors, so that

... among them Pallas Athena roused unquenchable laughter, and turned their wits awry. And now they laughed with alien lips, and bedabbled with blood was the flesh they ate, and their eyes were filled with tears and their spirits set on wailing. Then among them spoke godlike Theoclymenus, "Wretches, what evil do you suffer? Your heads are shrouded in night and your faces and your knees beneath you. Kindled is the sound of wailing, your cheeks are bathed in tears and the walls sprinkled with blood and the fair rafters. The porch and the court are filled with ghosts that hasten down to Erebus beneath the darkness, and the sun has perished from heaven and an evil mist hovers over all. (*Od.* 20.345–57)

Having fulfilled his purpose, Theoclymenus leaves the palace and disappears. The suitors, mad with wine, blood, meat, sex, and pride, only burst out laughing all the more, never suspecting that they have eaten their last meal on earth.

"Contest of the Bow" (Book 21)

All is prepared for the big recognition, when through the test of skill and strength the true king is revealed. It is unfortunately impossible to understand just how Homer envisioned the archery contest. The most puzzling part of his description is that the arrow needed to pass "through all 12 axes" (21.76) or "through the iron" (21.97). How can an arrow pass through the iron? A common explanation is that 12 ax-heads were buried in the earthen floor in a trench, blade down with their haft-holes up and in a line, and in this sense he fired "through the iron." If so, the shot would have to be fired very near the ground, with the archer squatting; it's probably not possible to make such a shot in the real world. A second common suggestion is that the axes were like Minoan double-axes, where the blades curve back dramatically toward the haft, forming a sort of open "O" resting on top of the haft. In this case the hafts would be fixed vertically in a line in the ground so that the O's at the top of each ax form a kind of tunnel. If so, what is the point of the trench? We also cannot be sure where the axes were set up, because if it was in the central hall (the megaron), then the hearth, so important in the story, will be in the center. Probably Homer did not himself understand the nature of the contest, whose original coherent explanation, now irrecoverable, became lost in the tradition.

Folktale heroes overcome their enemies with special weapons, just as Odysseus blinded the Cyclops with a special fire-hardened stake (instead of the sword he carried). Here the special weapon is a bow that once belonged to Iphitus, the son of the legendary great archer Eurytus. Heracles killed Iphitus when Iphitus came to his house in search of some stolen mares. For this terrible crime against *xenia*, Heracles paid a heavy price, according to later tradition: he was sold as a slave to a queen of Lydia. As Iphitus suffered from violated *xenia*, now will his bow take vengeance against those who have committed the same crime.

A quick recognition scene in the courtyard between Odysseus and the faithful Philoetius and Eumaeus, based again on the token of the scar, brings these men into the plot. There are now four against the 100-plus suitors.

The effete young men are pathetic in their efforts to handle a real weapon owned by a real man. Antinous, seeing how his companions fail, avoids embarrassment by suggesting that they stop the contest and give themselves up to drink: even so did the Cyclops drink before Odysseus overcame him. Narrative tension runs high as Penelope defends the beggar's right to give the bow a try, although she certainly is not going to marry him! Eumaeus picks it up to give it to Odysseus, then puts it down at the clamor of the suitors, then under threats from Telemachus picks it up again.

Odysseus inspects the bow, then strings it effortlessly – like a singer putting a new string to his lyre, Homer observes strikingly. Certainly Homer plucked the string of his lyre here to make the point, making it a rare occasion when we can reconstruct the poem's musical accompaniment. Odysseus' shot is a sure one, but the monster with 120 mouths, drunken and stupid like Polyphemus, even now does not understand that it is about to die.

"Slaughter of the Suitors" (Book 22)

Odysseus, like Superman, strips off his rags and with spellbinding speed throws the quiver of arrows at his feet. His appearance is like that of a god, an epiphany. This is the danger of violating *xenia*, because sometimes the stranger *is* a god. The first suitor, the leader Antinous, dies, an arrow through his throat as he drinks from a golden cup, and his blood mingles with the blood of the meat he's been eating. Still the young and the dumb, in their drunken madness, do not recognize Odysseus or realize what is happening. Before their execution they have a right to know why they are dying. There is right and wrong, and criminals like Aegisthus and Clytemnestra – and now the suitors – must pay for their deeds:

> You dogs, you thought that I would never more come home from the land of the Trojans, so you wasted my house and forced the maids to sleep with you and while yet I lived you courted my wife, having no fear of the gods who hold broad heaven nor of the future indignation of men. Now over you one and all are the cords of destruction made fast. (*Od.* 22.35–41)

The other leader, Eurymachus, feebly tries to blame it all on Antinous, as if Odysseus hadn't been in the house with them and suffered direct abuse from Eurymachus himself. His offer of recompense is similar to Agamemnon's to Achilles in the *Iliad*, or to that of the Cyclops when he wishes to persuade the fleeing Odysseus to come back to his cave and receive *xenia*. Appeal is useless. Right must triumph over wrong, justice over injustice.

Only against a gang of cowards and soft youths could four men, three of whom have never been in a fight and two of whom are slaves, hope to overcome 120 men. The arrows run out and the spear fight begins. Telemachus, who has tasted first blood by spearing a man in the back, fetches armor from the storeroom. In this scene we meet our greatest perplexities about the layout of Odysseus' house, because although Odysseus is standing on the threshold, the treacherous servant Melantheus somehow goes up and down the stairs without Odysseus seeing him. Penelope's room must be up the stairs, evidently off the same corridor as the storeroom. There is also a back door to the hall that seems to lead into the court, or to the space between the house and the wall of the court, through which a postern door leads outside to the town. Eumaeus covers this postern door during the early part of the battle. In any event, Philoetius and Eumaeus capture Melantheus in the storeroom and hog tie him for later mutilation. Nothing can be too bad for this villain.

Athena has been controlling events in the poem (except in the adventures) and has promised to support her favorite in his hour of need. Here she appears briefly as Mentor, urging Odysseus to try harder as she deflects the spears of suitors, 12 of whom Melantheus has armed from the storeroom. Still, the brunt of the battle must be borne by the city-sacker, the man of many turns, the man of much *mêtis*, and by his son, who once was a boy but now is a man.

With some charm, Homer has Telemachus spare Phemius the *aoidos*, who was forced to sing against his will, and who now pleads for his life to Odysseus:

> By your knees I beg you, Odysseus, and do you respect me and have pity, on your own self shall sorrow come hereafter if you kill the *aoidos*, I mean me, who sing to gods and men. Self-taught am I and the god has planted in my heart all kinds of songs. I am ready to sing to you as to a god. So do not be eager to cut my throat. (*Od.* 22.344–9)

Otherwise, only the "herald," a kind of errand boy, is spared.

Twelve faithless maids (including presumably Melantho) are forced to clean up the mess. They drag out the corpses and stack them in piles in the courtyard, which since the morning has become an abattoir and now a charnel house for the finest of the local nobility. Odysseus tells his son to put the maids to the sword, but in a scene of exquisite cruelty Telemachus hangs them in a row from a ship's cable attached to a column and to a *tholos*, a round building in the court not previously mentioned. From this cable they wiggle and bounce, "but not for long" (22.473). No ingenuity has explained just how this execution took place, but its very vagueness and abruptness heightens its horror. Odysseus commands that sulfur be burned in the hall. Sulfur is repulsive to ghosts and maleficent spirits, of which there are likely to be a rich supply, hovering nearby.

"Recognition of Odysseus and Penelope" (Book 23)

Homer's wry humor is strong in his presentation of the sometimes daft Penelope, crazy like a fox, whose persona of someone not paying very much attention to what is going on has been key to her survival for a long time in dangerous conditions. Earlier, when Eurycleia dropped the great bronze bowl in the dusky hallway, Penelope noticed not a thing, and now Eurycleia awakes her in her chamber from a nap that was the most restful she's had in years. Eurycleia delivers the astounding news. While she enjoyed her sleep, her husband came home and killed the suitors. Neither this deed, nor report of the scar, persuades the cautious and crafty Penelope.

Telemachus, who began the poem complaining about his mother's behavior, now calls her cold as stone, as is anyone who can sit beside her long-lost husband and not see that it is he. He leaves them alone when Penelope concedes that whoever this man is (and surely it is not her husband) he can sleep in Odysseus' bed, and Eurycleia will bring the bed right out. By this token Penelope tricks Odysseus into revealing his true identity: he built the bed himself and one post was an olive tree that grew into the ground. The floor of the palace bedchamber must be packed earth and on the ground floor, whereas Penelope's room is up the stairs, but exactly where in relationship to the main hall is unclear.

Recognized by his wife, Odysseus retires with Penelope to the bed to make love, while Phemius plays and Odysseus' followers (who are they?) dance in the court. Passersby would think that a wedding was taking place, as in fact it is – Penelope has re-wed her own true man. While in bed Odysseus summarizes his adventures on the high seas, taking care to explain away his year in Circe's bed: "Then he told of all the wiles and craftiness of Circe . . ." (*Od.* 23.321).

Some commentators, ancient and modern, have thought that the *Odyssey* originally ended at line 24.296 with the reunion of husband and wife, but too much remains unsolved for that. Although Odysseus is now husband to his wife and lord of his house, he is yet to be son to his father and king of the land. To this end, next morning, he and Telemachus and the others strap on armor and take up spears to face the trouble that must surely come.

"Suitors in the Underworld" (24.1–204), "Recognition of Odysseus and Laertes" (24.205–411), and "Odysseus, King of Ithaca" (24.412–548)

In a sharp jump-shift Homer takes us to the underworld. Hermes guides the spirits of the suitors to the fields of asphodel. There they come on the *psychai* of Agamemnon and Achilles conversing with one another. Agamemnon describes Achilles' glorious funeral, a good example of how the *Odyssey* tidies up details left over from the *Iliad*, where Achilles is still alive. Because the *Odyssey* refers to the *Iliad* in this self-conscious way, and not the other way around, all believe that the *Odyssey* is later than the *Iliad*. Agamemnon, whose story was set as a parallel to that of Odysseus in the first lines of the poem, complains of his fate, the opposite to that of Odysseus. Well, once again, *cherchez la femme*.

Agamemnon asks the suitor Amphimedon what has happened, and for the third time we hear the story of Penelope's web. As Homer summarized in outline form Odysseus' adventures in his pillow talk with Penelope, here he summarizes the story of the return of Odysseus. Amphimedon thinks that Penelope was in the plot from the beginning, but we know she was not.

In the meantime Odysseus has found his aged and ailing father Laertes in the orchard. Odysseus torments him with reminiscence about his lost son, tells a brand new lying tale, claiming now to be from Sicily, then reveals himself through the scar and through the memory of trees that Laertes gave him. And just in time, for the townspeople now know what has happened.

Many critics have complained about the slack ending of the *Odyssey*, but a slack ending is Homer's style. The ending of the *Iliad* is slack: "So they buried horse-taming Hector." You cannot kill the flower of the islands without consequences, and when the families of the dead suitors, led by the father of the main suitor Antinous, attack Odysseus and now nine other men, Laertes, invigorated by his son's return, puts a spear through the man's brains. The gods stand behind every event of this poem, and at Athena's urging Zeus drops a thunderbolt between the two groups. That brings them up short. Odysseus has returned. He is husband to Penelope. He is lord of Ithaca, a bad land for horses. The story is over.

6

Conclusion and Summary

Modern literatures do not begin with Homer, because Homer comes from somewhere. He could not have existed without a Mesopotamian tradition of storytelling that was thousands of years old by the time of the Greek Iron Age. He also owed much to native Greek traditions and to the social power of a warrior aristocracy, who valued the past as an exemplar for the present and who saw the past as a time when their own ancestors fought in the Trojan War or in the war against Thebes. After all, Greek aristocrats obtained their power in society through martial prowess and superior "virtue" (Latin *virtus* = "manliness"). When a warrior goes directly against the enemy, to die or kill, his friends know about it and respect him for his manliness. When the only certainty to life is its end (perhaps a gruesome end), at least a man can act like a man and face the death that is sure to come. All warriors are bound by the same understanding. No one knows what the common man thinks, except for the scurrilous outburst of the reprehensible Thersites, who is ridiculed and beaten as an example for anyone else with a similar repulsive desire to "strive against big men [*basileis*]" (*Il.* 2.247). No such loose and internally egalitarian aristocracy as the Greek warrior class existed in the ancient Near East, where the staggering wealth generated by irrigation agriculture along the Tigris, Euphrates, and Nile had long before created a society of intense class division.

Homer's Complementary Poems

The *Iliad* is about men at war. From the beginning of the species, whenever that was, war has been the male's prerogative. There is no thought that there might be a world without war – that would be ridiculous – but its suffering stands in contrast to the gentle ways of peace, when Trojan women wash their linen at the troughs that run hot and cold, past which Achilles chases Hector to his death. War is what men do and where they die in ghastly ways, while the women await their own fates as widows or are taken by the rough hands of captors who will rape and enslave them. Zeus, as Achilles recalls in the "Ransom of Hector," gives to some all evil, but others receive some good along with the evil. In its hardheaded no-holds-barred pessimism about mortal struggle the *Iliad* was about real life, and still is.

We enjoy studying the *Iliad* because we recognize the world it portrays. Fear is the enemy of all, as we learn in numerous pep talks, but the warrior overcomes his fear. He is a realist. In the *Iliad* this heroic code, as it is called, has run afoul of the emerging state in which power and respect do not depend entirely on manliness, but on the agreement that centralized power is for the common good. On Agamemnon's argument was built the monstrous modern tyrannies of Stalin and Hitler. Certainly Achilles doesn't like what the emerging state means to him: his humiliation.

We may agree that Agamemnon is first among equals, but he acts like a thief to establish his manliness at the expense of another, when his authority as statesman must have a different basis. Agamemnon's behavior is otherwise intolerable. He gives in to anger when trapped into giving back his war-captive; statesmen should not give in to anger. He throws his weight around recklessly, like a madman, smashing things left and right. Only calm could save Achilles, but Achilles, too, is a man of anger. His character equals his fate. He claims that he could choose another course, a long obscure life with family back in Phthia instead of glory and an early death and song in the ears of men, but he really has no choice and he never did.

That is why Agamemnon's hideous behavior shakes Achilles to the foundation. Achilles stands for freedom. Agamemnon takes away his glory through the arbitrary power of the nascent state. Achilles cannot kill him (though he is tempted to do so) if he wishes ever to reestablish his *timê*, and Athena assures him of this. While Agamemnon behaves in a disgraceful fashion, Achilles' so-called friends stand around and gawk. They are as guilty as Agamemnon in a conspiracy to take away every shred of purpose from Achilles' life.

As a man of anger Achilles pursues Hector and kills him. Not until Priam comes to his tent does he abandon his anger, at the story's resolution. He might have killed Priam and even should have done so: here is the father of the man who killed his friend. He doesn't kill him because he sees that in their sorrow they are the same. They weep together, eat together, and at least for that moment, the anger is gone. The story comes to an end. It's not the moral "don't be angry" that thrills us, but the spectacle of a man who has achieved understanding about the unity of human life.

In the *Iliad* aristocrats clash in the game of honor, but in the *Odyssey* one male alone goes up against the world and against death itself, which will swallow Achilles in an instant. And Odysseus survives. Odysseus never gives in to anger, but swallows his furious resentments, planning through stealth to gain victory. And gain it he does.

With astonishing sophistication and skill Homer blends the folktale hero who fights monsters and resists beautiful women with the Trojan-fighter who through martial prowess destroys the enemy. He manages this conflation by placing in Odysseus' own mouth tales of his folktale encounters, setting them at one remove in the narrative. Antinous explicitly compares him to an *aoidos* who holds the audience entranced. A pervasive theme in the *Odyssey* is the greatness of song and its central place in culture whereas, except for the obscure Thamyris mentioned in the "Catalogue of Ships," there seem to be no *aoidoi* in the *Iliad* (Achilles sings of the "glorious deeds of men" to the accompaniment of a lyre (*Il.* 9.189), but Achilles is no *aoidos*).

The adventures in the *Odyssey* take place in a fairyland where things do not work as they do here. On Circe's island you cannot tell where the sun rises and sets. The land of the Phaeacians, where the *aoidic* Odysseus sings his song, stands on a middle ground, still a fairy king-dom with lifelike metal animals standing before the doors and magic ships that steer themselves, but without cannibals and monsters and brash seducers. Finally, Ithaca is what we might call the real world (although there is still room for goddesses in disguise). In broad terms, Odysseus' journey takes him into the world of symbols and the world of ghosts, then back through a halfway house to the humdrum barbarities of Iros the beggar, the lowlife Melantheus, and the crude appetites of young men without wisdom.

A central theme in Odysseus' journey to the middle of the ocean and back to hearth and kin is the death and rebirth of the hero, but by extension his journey is that of all males. Odysseus goes into caves, falls asleep, and is allured by song and woman. His victory, marked by recognition and the pronouncing of his name, is always new life. In the end he takes a wife and rules his house.

Achilles awaits death's extinction, the logical consequence of the choices he makes. He is obsessed with the meaning of his behavior and thus indifferent to the material world, to the prizes of Agamemnon or the ransom of Priam. Odysseus defies death and is out to get rich. Treasure is life, and he brings home an enormous quantity of it from the Phaeacians, more than he might have brought from Troy. Although anxious to return, Odysseus would gladly have spent an extra year on Scheria, he once tells us, if that would have increased his haul. Yet he places the treasure in a cave and forgets all about it. The greatest treasure is still ahead: the house, its flocks and slaves, and the delights of family life and the power of social control. In such securities Achilles has only theoretical interest.

Truly, the *Iliad* and the *Odyssey* form a sort of whole, the one questioning the basis for values we accept without question, the other affirming the values of property and family and continuing life. Constantly the *Odyssey* fills in gaps in the narrative of the *Iliad*, gives us the end of the story. We learn what happened to Agamemnon and Menelaus and Nestor and the lesser Ajax (son of Oileus) and the greater Ajax (son of Telamon). We learn about the death of Achilles and even speak with him in the other world. We hear the story of the Trojan Horse and how the war came to an end. We see Helen settled back at home, still in control with her charm and her drugs. Once scholars thought that the "*Odyssey* poet" was influenced by the "*Iliad* poet," and consciously set out to complete his tale. The poet best able to do that was Homer himself. He gives us in his two poems an integrated vision of human life in all its terror, sweetness, and complexity.

Homer's Imitators

Such qualities have made Homer's poems "classics" that everyone agrees are worth studying. However, the unprecedented scope, complexity, and length of the *Iliad* and the *Odyssey* precluded any direct imitations for a long time. We mentioned earlier the Cyclic Poems – hexameter poems on heroic themes taken down by dictation from other *aoidoi* in the seventh, sixth, and maybe even the fifth centuries BC, with Trojan themes or built around the sack of seven-gated Thebes. Lost today, the

Cyclic Poems were better known to Greeks of the Archaic Period than either the *Iliad* or the *Odyssey* and inspired many standard scenes on illustrated Greek pottery. One poem told of the sack of Troy; another of events leading up to the *Iliad* all the way back to the Judgment of Paris. Some, but not all, of the Cyclic Poems were attributed to Homer, so that when Aeschylus (525–456 BC) said that his plays were "slices from the banquet of Homer," he meant that he was stealing plots from these Cyclic Poems, not from the *Iliad* and the *Odyssey*, in which Aeschylus had little interest.

We don't know very much about the Cyclic Poems. Summaries survive, but otherwise only scattered lines. Above all we don't know in what relation they stood to the texts of the Homeric poems. Although they appear to fill in gaps left by the *Iliad* and the *Odyssey* in telling the whole saga of Troy, and although the Greeks themselves understood the Cyclic Poems in this way, it is probable that some or all of these poems were taken down independently of any knowledge of the texts of Homer's poems. One poem, the so-called *Little Iliad*, certainly repeated events in the extant long *Iliad* and we can be sure of other overlaps. We have too little information for reliable conclusions, but we don't usually think of the Cyclic Poems as "imitating" the *Iliad* and the *Odyssey*.

Imitation is a prerogative of a fully literate tradition. Certainly Apollonius of Rhodes, who lived in Alexandria, Egypt, in the third century BC, 500 years after Homer, belonged to such a tradition and he did imitate Homer's poems in a conscious way, the first we know to have done this. By then, conditions of life in the ancient Mediterranean had changed utterly. Thanks to the military success of Alexander, the intellectual leaders of the Hellenic tradition were living in a foreign land The *aoidoi* were long since extinct, as were the village aristocracies that they served. Apollonius of Rhodes learned his poetry from books and knew nothing about the oral origins of Homer's poems. He faced the transmitted texts as literary classics worthy of hard study, close attention, and admiring imitation.

For Apollonius, Homer had defined the genre of epic: a long poem about adventure and war in which the gods intervene and heroes wear ornamental epithets in a six-beat line made of dactyls and spondees. Apollonius imitated Homer in his *Argonautica*, the story of Jason's journey to Colchis to recover the Golden Fleece, his love affair with the witch Medea, and his problems in returning home. Apollonius thought of himself as writing in a Homeric style, but his epithets, for example, are merely ornamental and obviously do not reflect oral composition. Apollonius introduced modern themes in his portrayal of Jason's weakness and Medea's strength. Apollonius' poem was probably never memorized for re-performance, as were Homer's, but was read aloud from a papyrus before an elite audience of learned men and women. The courts where Homer sang were surrounded with mud-brick walls, but Alexandria was the capital of one of the most powerful monarchies ever, drenched in wealth and driven by cultural ambition.

Alexandria's poets and intellectuals succeeded so well in their ambition to determine taste and foster achievement in culture that when the Roman elite expropriated Greek literature for themselves they took its Alexandrian form, including the now-literate genre of epic composition. In the third century BC the Roman Livius Andronicus translated the *Odyssey* into Latin, the first major poem in Latin (now lost), but when Vergil (70–19 BC) came to write his great *Aeneid*, his model was as much Apollonius as Homer. For example, Aeneas' love affair with Dido evokes and is modeled on Jason's affair with Medea. Vergil also imitated Apollonius in his obsession with stylistic elegance, refined expression, and conscious demands on the education of his cultured audience. The first words of the *Aeneid* are *arma virumque cano,* "of arms and the man I sing," which deliberately invoke the *Iliad,* war, and the *Odyssey,* whose first word in Greek is "man." Vergil expected his audience to notice the allusion, the first of thousands in the poem, whose meaning is enriched by the whole of written classical literature standing behind it – a backdrop and sounding board for the story of Aeneas' flight across water (= the *Odyssey*) and the conquest of Italy (= the *Iliad*). On the surface, and in English translation, the *Aeneid* and Homer's poems look somewhat alike, and one does depend on the others; they are all long poems on heroic themes. Yet the Alexandrian *Aeneid* is utterly different in *what* it means and *how* it means.

It wasn't so much Homer's prestige as Vergil's that inspired such other Latin epics as the *Pharsalia* of Lucan (AD 39–65), about the Roman civil war, and the *Thebaid* of Statius (AD 45–96), about the legend of the Seven against Thebes. During the Renaissance Vergil's powerful model inspired Italian epics and earned him the right to guide Dante into the underworld and up the mountain of Purgatory. In England, such works as Milton's *Paradise Lost* (1667) imitate Vergil in style and convention.

In modern times the epic is a dead form, although we may speak of an "epic" film, like *Star Wars,* or an "epic" novel, like *War and Peace.* That is only metaphor. It is striking how all of Homer's imitators, except Vergil, are today never read for pleasure, or even read at all except by a handful of scholars in select universities. Homer, by contrast, is read avidly and never more widely than today, although torn from his oral roots, his language, and his environment. No doubt his greatness is a mystery, but one we are grateful for.

Notes

1 Paper, unknown to the ancient Western world, is made by breaking up wood into fiber, immersing the fibers in water, and allowing them to matt on a screen; the Arabs brought this very early Chinese invention to the West in the eighth century AD.

2 F. A. Wolf, *Prolegomena to Homer*, trans. A. Grafton, G. W. Most, and J. E. G. Zetzel (Princeton, NJ, 1985), p. 101.

3 Ibid: p. 79.

4 J. Russo, M. Fernandez-Galiano, and A. Heubeck, eds., *A Commentary on Homer's Odyssey Vol. 3: Books XVII–XXIV* (English edition, Oxford, 1992), p. 131.

5 By Levant I mean Canaan–Syria, the strip of land from northern Phoenicia to Gaza, then inland to the Bika valley in the north, enclosed by the Lebanon and anti-Lebanon ranges, and to the Negev Desert in the south.

6 In historical times the great Zulu leader Shaka of the nineteenth century (d. 1828) created a style of fighting similar to the ancient Greek *phalanx* in armor and tactics and quickly overwhelmed all who came against him.

7 From William W. Hallo and K. Lawson Younger, Jr., eds., *The Context of Scripture: Canonical Compositions from the Biblical World* (Leiden, 1997), p. 250.

8 In fact Homer does tell the story when the nurse Eurycleia recognizes him from the token of the scar (*Od.* 19.428ff.). Either Aristotle had a different text, or he is being careless, as often.

9 There are two Ajaxes in the poem, one the son of Telamon and often called "greater Ajax" or "the greater Ajax," the other the son of Oileus, called "the lesser Ajax." Simply "Ajax" is the son of Telamon. Homer often refers to the "two Ajaxes," using the dual grammatical number, but he seems sometimes to mean by this (1) the greater and the lesser Ajax or (2) the greater Ajax and his half-brother Teucer, the archer.

10   In modern film entertainment, by contrast, where the audience is between 18 and 36 years old, the common plot shows the young as vigorous and in love while their middle-aged parents, libidinous and corrupt, oppose them; in the end, the young triumph over the old.

11   Aeolus is also the name of the apparently unrelated founder of the House of Iolcus, from which Jason was descended.

Further Reading

The bibliography on Homer is gigantic and no one reads it all. Much of it is technical or dull. In the following I will highlight books and sources in English that are relatively easy to find and that will aid the beginning student to explore the endless maze of Homeric studies. I begin with studies of general interest, then studies relevant to the two poems.

Translations, Texts

Few today read all or even large parts of Homer in Greek. Fortunately, a new fashion in translation, begun in the mid-twentieth century at the University of Chicago, has generated numerous superior translations. Richmond Lattimore's *Iliad* (Chicago, IL, 1951) and *Odyssey* (Chicago, IL, 1965) remain the most Homeric and best give the feel of Homer's formulaic Greek. Robert Fitzgerald's translations are livelier and freer and his *Odyssey* (New York, 1961) is especially delightful. Recently, Robert Fagles' translations of the *Iliad* (New York, 1990) and the *Odyssey* (New York, 1999) have attracted many admirers. Other good translations of both poems include those by Stanley Lombardo: his *Iliad* (Indianapolis, IN, 1997) and *Odyssey* (Indianapolis, IN, 2000) are in a vigorous, modern American style.

Two good books accompany translations and well educate the Greekless student in the complexities of the two poems: J. C. Hogan's *A Guide to the Iliad: Based on the Translation by Robert Fitzgerald* (New York, 1979) and R. Hexter's *A Guide to the Odyssey: A Commentary on the English Translation by Robert Fitzgerald* (New York, 1993).

The Greek texts are usually read in the Oxford Classical Texts *Homeri opera* edited by T. W. Allen and later D. B. Munro and published in various editions between 1902 and 1920. In 1998–2000 there appeared a fine new text by M. L. West, *Homerus Ilias* (Munich/Leipzig), unfortunately not easy to obtain.

General Studies

Two good general surveys by a collection of experts are *A Companion to Homer* edited by A. J. B. Wace and F. H. Stubbings (London, 1962) and *A New Companion to Homer* edited by B. B. Powell and I. Morris (Leiden, 1995). Wace and Stubbings reflect heavily what used to be called Homeric archeology: the relationship between archeological finds from the Bronze Age (taken to be Homer's world) and the poems. We now think Homer's world is the eighth century BC. Nonetheless these studies are interesting, and there are excellent essays on the Homeric Question and technical descriptions of Homeric language. The Powell and Morris collection is modern, with an essay on almost every topic, and with much less archeology and more literary, cultural, and historical studies.

A thorough if sometimes stodgy overview of Homeric criticism is provided in G. S Kirk's *The Songs of Homer* (Cambridge, 1962), later abbreviated as *Homer and the Oral Tradition* (Cambridge, 1976). H. Fraenkel, *Early Greek Poetry and Philosophy*, translated by M. Hadas and J. Willis (New York, 1973), discusses the singers and their epics, language, verse, style, gods, and other topics. W. G. Thalmann, in *Conventions of Form and Thought in Early Greek Poetry* (Baltimore, MD, 1984), places Homer into broader contexts of archaic poetry.

Many general studies offer plot summaries, but they all follow similar lines. C. Whitman's *Homer and the Heroic Tradition* (Cambridge, MA, 1958) identifies complex patterns of ring composition and parallel presentations of themes within the *Iliad*, which it compares to Geometric pottery. C. R. Beye, in *Ancient Epic Poetry* (Ithaca, NY, 1993), brings wisdom and experience to a study of the Greco-Roman epic tradition. A succinct overview of the Cyclic Poems is provided in M. Davies, *The Epic Cycle* (Bristol, 1989). P. Toohey, in *Reading Epic: An Introduction to the Ancient Narratives* (London, 1992), is good on genre and includes a chapter on Apollonius' *Argonautica*. Widely read but employing an inappropriate etymologizing method and slippery in its understanding of oral theory is G. Nagy's *The Best of the Achaeans: Concepts of the Hero in Archaic Greek Poetry* (Baltimore, MD, 1979).

Commentaries

There are recent line-by-line commentaries in English for both poems. For the *Iliad*, G. S. Kirk has served as general editor of a massive six-volume commentary, *The Iliad: A Commentary* (Cambridge, 1985–93), with volumes by Kirk, J. B. Hainsworth, R. Janko, M. Edwards, and N. Richardson. Each volume contains good introductory essays, although Kirk's notion of a "memorized" oral text is fantasy. For the *Odyssey* there is a good although sometimes curiously old-fashioned *Commentary on Homer's Odyssey* (Oxford, 1988–92) with contributions by A. Heubeck, S. West, J. B. Hainsworth, A. Hoekstra, J. Russo, and M. Fernández Galiano. W. B. Stanford's commentary, though old, is always useful: *Odyssey*, 2 vols., 2nd edn. (London, 1959). I. De Jong's *A Narratological Commentary on the Odyssey* (Cambridge, 2001) is a line-by-line exploration of narrative art, character, plot, and the type scene.

History of Text

M. Haslam offers a superior history of the early text in "Homeric Papyri and the Transmission of the Text" in B. B. Powell and I. Morris, *A New Companion to Homer* (Leiden, 1995), pp. 55–100. M. L. West's *Studies in the Text and Transmission of the Iliad* (Munich/Leipzig, 2001), by a foremost scholar, is a thorough up-to-date study. R. Janko's influential *Homer, Hesiod and the Hymns: Diachronic Development in Epic Diction* (Cambridge, 1982) establishes a date of around 730 BC for the *Iliad*, somewhat later for the *Odyssey* (probably too late).

Homeric Question, Parry/Lord

F. A. Wolf's eighteenth-century Latin presents a challenge, but fortunately a modern English translation is *Prolegomena to Homer*, translated by A. Grafton, G. W. Most, and J. E. G. Zetzel (Princeton, NJ, 1985), with a good introduction that explains Wolf's debt to contemporary biblical scholars.

Adam Parry, son of Milman Parry, gathered his father's papers together in *The Making of Homeric Verse: The Collected Papers of Milman Parry*, ed. A. Parry (Oxford, 1971; reprinted New York, 1980). Milman Parry's writings are brilliant technical analyses of language, but you need to know Greek. Adam Parry's introduction to this volume is probably the best short introduction to what Milman Parry was trying to say. The introduction is included in A. Parry's *The Language of Achilles and Other Papers*, foreword by P. H. J. Lloyd-Jones (Oxford, 1989), which also contains A. Parry's important essay "Have We Homer's *Iliad*?" in which he shows how there can be no intermediary between the words of the song as Homer sang it and the text we have today.

A. B. Lord's seminal *The Singer of Tales* (Cambridge, MA, 1960) was reissued with a terrific CD-ROM showing many pictures of *guslars* and even a film clip of Avdo Mejedovich singing: see the second edition edited by S. Mitchell and G. Nagy (Cambridge, MA, 2000). Numerous books by Lord's follower, J. M. Foley, illustrate the contemporary state of the oral/formulaic theory, for example *The Theory of Oral Composition: History and Methodology* (Bloomington, IN, 1988) and *Traditional Oral Epic: The Odyssey, Beowulf, and the Serbo-Croatian Return Song* (Berkeley, CA, 1990).

Archery at the Dark of the Moon by N. Austin (Berkeley, CA, 1975) argues against the impression that formulas are mechanical and without semantic connotation. M. N. Nagler attempts to deal with the conundrum of the indefinable formula in *Spontaneity and Tradition: A Study in the Oral Art of Homer* (Berkeley, CA, 1974) by supposing that they ride on a subconscious *Gestalt*, much as does ordinary language.

Some of Parry's field material is published in M. Parry, A. B. Lord, and D. E. Bynum, eds., *Serbo-Croatian Heroic Songs* (Cambridge, MA, and Belgrade, 1953), including Avdo Mejedovich's *The Wedding of Smailagich Meho*, as long as the *Odyssey*. Descriptions of the *guslars* and transcriptions of conversations with them provide invaluable insights.

Technological Background, the Alphabet

There is a straightforward history of papyrus in R. Parkinson and S. Quirke, *Papyrus* (Austin, TX, 1995). The importance of clay as a substrate is emphasized in E. Chiera, *They Wrote on Clay: The Babylonian Tablets Speak Today*, edited by G. Cameron (Chicago, IL, 1956), one of the best introductions to writing in Mesopotamia.

The classic study of writing, never surpassed, is I. J. Gelb's *A Study of Writing* (Chicago, IL, 1963). A good recent overview is A. Robinson, *The Story of Writing* (New York, 1999). The best book on West Semitic inscriptions is J. Naveh's *Early History of the Alphabet* (Jerusalem and Leiden, 1982), also typical in its confusion about the relationship of the Greek alphabet to the earlier West Semitic syllabic systems.

R. Carpenter established the means of dating the invention of the Greek alphabet in a landmark article, "The Antiquity of the Greek Alphabet," *American Journal of Archaeology* 37 (1933), 8–29. Many Semitists (e.g., Naveh), calling West Semitic writing "alphabetic," think that the transmission could have happened almost any time, even in the Bronze Age.

I have been interested in the relationship between the history of the Greek alphabet and the date of the Homeric texts, best represented in my *Homer and the Origin of the Greek Alphabet* (Cambridge, 1991), where I argue that the Greek alphabet was devised to create these texts. I came to this thesis independently, but was anticipated in part by the British scholar H. T. Wade-Gery, *The Poet of the Iliad* (Cambridge, 1952), a short book with original interpretations. In my *Writing and the Origins of Greek Literature* (Cambridge, 2002) I examine the place of the Homeric poems within the theory and history of writing.

Homer and History

Important books that advocated the "Bronze Age Homer" are M. P. Nilsson, *Homer and Mycenae* (London, 1933) and T. B. L. Webster, *From Mycenae to Homer* (London, 1958). J. V. Luce, *Homer and the Heroic Age* (London, 1975), astutely compares the poems with archeological data, with excellent illustrations. D. L. Page's brilliant (but often mistaken) *History and the Homeric Iliad* (Berkeley, CA, 1959) combines archeological and documentary evidence with original philological investigation. The best summary of the problem is J. Bennet's "Homer and the Bronze Age," in *A New Companion to Homer* edited by B. B. Powell and I. Morris (Leiden, 1995), pp. 511–34. M. I. Finley, *The World of Odysseus*, 2nd edn. (London, 1977), pushed Homer's world out of the Bronze Age into the ninth and tenth centuries BC. I. Morris wrote an influential article that placed Homer's world still later, in the eighth century BC: "The Use and Abuse of Homer," *Classical Antiquity* 6 (1986), 81–138, a conclusion accepted by most.

For a good collection of essays on the evolution of the *polis*, see L. Mitchell and P. J. Rhodes, eds., *The Development of the Polis in Archaic Greece* (London, 1996), especially K. Raaflaub's "Evolution of the Early Greek Polis." A good essay on the age of colonial expansion is provided by J. Graham in "The Colonial Expansion of Greece," in the *Cambridge Ancient History*, vol. 3, 2nd edn. (Cambridge, 1982), pp. 83–162. J. Boardman's *The Greeks Overseas*, 2nd edn. (London, 1980), is a fine overview. I. Malkin's *The Returns of Odysseus* (Berkeley, CA, 1999) places the poem in the context of Western colonization.

The Euboeans, Greece's earliest colonizers, had a special role in the formation of the Homeric texts. For the warrior burial at Lefkandi, see M. R. Popham, E. Touloupa, and L. H. Sackett, "The Hero of Lefkandi," *Antiquity* 56 (1982), 159–64. Evidence for Euboean dialect in Homer is found in M. L. West's "The Rise of the Greek Epic," *Journal of Hellenic Studies* 108 (1988), 151–72. D. Ridgway summarizes evidence for Euboean exploration in Italy in the eighth century BC, to which the *Odyssey* owes much, in *The First Western Greeks* (Cambridge, 1992). O. Murray's *Early Greece*, 2nd edn. (London, 1993), is excellent in general for social and historical background and emphasizes the importance of the Euboeans as Greek cultural leaders in the early eighth century BC. Important, too, is the essay "Homer, History, and Archaeology" by J. P. Crielaard, in *Homeric Questions* (Amsterdam, 1995), pp. 201–88, which also contains excellent essays by other scholars (but in French).

H. L. Lorimer's *Homer and the Monuments* (London, 1950), sympathetic to the Bronze Age Homer, is still an important study comparing Homer with material culture. Lorimer has a chapter on "Arms and Armour" (pp. 132–335), a detailed interpretation of the evidence up to 1950 and a starting point for much subsequent discussion in English. A. M. Snodgrass covers post-Bronze Age weaponry in *Early Greek Armour and Weapons: From the End of the Bronze Age to 600 BC* (Edinburgh, 1964), including separate chapters on different elements of the panoply and a discussion of literary evidence. Good on warfare generally is H. van Wees, *Status Warriors: War, Violence, and Society in Homer and History* (Amsterdam, 1992).

Homer and Art

K. Friis Johansen's *The Iliad in Early Greek Art* (Copenhagen, 1967) established the predominance of themes from the Cyclic poets in the seventh and sixth centuries BC over themes from the *Iliad* and the *Odyssey*. A. M. Snodgrass's *Homer and the Artists: Text and Picture in Early Greek Art* (Cambridge, 1998) is a recent competent survey, but too reluctant to tie art to text. In my own *Writing and the Origins of Greek Literature* (Cambridge, 2002) I show how Eastern images inspired new myths in Greece, making for desperate complexity in sorting out the relationship between myth and art. D. Buitron and B. Cohen, eds., *The Odyssey in Ancient Art: An Epic in Word and Image* (Annandale-on-Hudson, NY, 1992), gathers early images relating to the *Odyssey*, with valuable essays. Two complementary books are M. J. Anderson's *The Fall of Troy in Early Greek Poetry and Art* (Oxford, 1997), which takes account of poetic inspiration from many sources, and S. Woodford's *The Trojan War in Ancient Art* (Ithaca, NY, 1993), which summarizes complex evidence for this popular theme.

Near East

Greece's indebtedness to Near Eastern literature is an old topic, but uniquely persuasive are W. Burkert's *The Orientalizing Revolution: Near Eastern Influence on Greek Culture in the Early Archaic Age*, translated by M. E. Pinder (Cambridge, MA, 1992) and M. L. West's exhaustive *The East Face of Helicon: West Asiatic Elements in Greek Poetry and Myth* (Oxford, 1997). There is an excellent introduction and translation of *Gilgamesh* in S. Dalley, *Myths from Mesopotamia* (Oxford, 1989). Translations of Ugaritic myths can be found in W. W. Hallo and K. Lawson Younger, Jr., eds., *The Context of Scripture: Canonical Compositions from the Biblical World* (Leiden, 1997), and in the third edition of the classic collection edited by J. B. Pritchard, *Ancient Near Eastern Texts Relating to the Old Testament* (Princeton, NJ, 1969). Many good recent books on the Phoenicians include M. E. Aubet, *The Phoenicians and the West*, translated by M. Turton (Cambridge, 1993).

Religion

Basic background for Homer's religion is in W. Burkert's *Greek Religion*, translated by J. Raffan (Cambridge, MA, 1985), and also important material in Burkert's *Structure and History of Greek Mythology and Ritual* (Berkeley, CA, 1979). J. Griffin's *Homer on Life and Death* (Oxford, 1980) has sound chapters on religion as well as other interesting interpretative material.

Readers, Style, Similes

H. Clarke's *Homer's Readers: A Historical Introduction to the Iliad and the Odyssey* (Newark, NJ, 1981) describes the reception of the Homeric poems from antiquity to the present, primarily reception by critics, not creative artists. Most general books about Homer (see above) discuss style at some point. A well-known essay about Homer's style is "Odysseus' Scar," the first chapter of E. Auerbach's classic *Mimesis* (New York, 1954), pp. 1–19, where he argues that Homeric style is characterized by externalized description, transparent meaning with the temporal setting in the foreground, no character development, legendary rather than historical sources, and a social perspective limited to the aristocracy. S. Weil's *The Iliad or the Poem of Force* is widely read as a study in destructive conflict, published in French in 1940 (translated by M. McCarthy, New York, 1945). Written as Hitler's armies marched, the essay about Europe's first war poet smells of Europe's greatest war.

An original recent commentator on Homer's style, with a linguistic approach, is E. Bakker, although his work can be technical. One may consult his edited collection, with A. Kahane, *Written Voices, Spoken Signs: Tradition, Performance, and the Epic Text* (Cambridge, MA, 1997), which contains an additional bibliography.

A good study of the simile can be found in C. Moulton, *Similes in the Homeric Poems* (Göttingen, 1977), which argues that similes are more than ornamentation or relief, but actually further narration.

The *Iliad*

Many excellent studies have explored the literary aspects of the poem. H. Bloom's edited *Homer's The Iliad* (New York, 1987) collects essays by leading scholars. M. S. Silk's *Homer: The Iliad* (Cambridge, 1987) is a brief and sensible introduction. E. T. Owen's *The Story of the Iliad* (Toronto, 1946) describes just what is happening in the narrative (not always obvious). M. Edwards' *Homer: Poet of the Iliad* (Baltimore, MD, 1988) is a superior introduction with book-by-book commentaries and an extensive bibliography.

G. Else's *Aristotle's Poetics: The Argument* (Cambridge, MA, 1963) thoroughly explores what Aristotle meant by plot. J. M. Redfield's *Nature and Culture in the Iliad: The Tragedy of Hector* (Chicago, IL, 1975) follows Aristotle in focusing on action (the logical probability or necessity of developments in the plot) rather than character. The premises for interpreting action are based on nature, culture, and their interrelationship, he thinks, and Achilles and Hector suffer tragedies that explicate the vulnerability of the hero on the borderline between nature and culture.

A. W. H. Adkins' *Merit and Responsibility: A Study in Greek Values* (Chicago, IL, 1960) is a powerful treatment of Homeric morality that laid the basis for further discussion. A broad review of major themes of the *Iliad* is found in S. Schein's *The Mortal Hero* (Berkeley, CA, 1984). Essays edited by J. Wright well represent Anglo-American criticism: see *Essays on the Iliad* (Bloomington, IN, 1978). O. Taplin's *Homeric Soundings: The Shaping of the Iliad* (Oxford, 1995) contains many insights about structure and meaning. R. Martin's *The Language of Heroes: Speech and Performance in the Iliad* (Ithaca, NY, 1989) has a discussion on speech used as a means to gain power in Homeric society.

Those who enjoy fictional recreations of Trojan saga will find pleasure in C. Wolf's *Cassandra*, translated from the German by Jan Van Heurck (New York, 1984), a feminist rewriting of the *Iliad* told by the scorned prophetess.

The *Odyssey*

In the ancient world the *Iliad* was far more popular than the *Odyssey*; three times as many papyrus fragments of the *Iliad* are found in Egypt as of the *Odyssey*. Perhaps modern taste prefers the *Odyssey* because of its strong theme of conflict and resolution between the sexes, and because it avoids long scenes of mind-numbing battle. In recent years many exceptional books on the *Odyssey* have been published and continue to be published. J. Griffin's *Homer: The Odyssey* (Cambridge, 1987), parallel to M. Silk's book on the *Iliad* (see above), covers the basic ground. S. V. Tracy's *The Story of the Odyssey* (Princeton, NJ, 1990) is written in parallel to E. T. Owen's summary of the *Iliad* (see above) and is as excellent.

Old, but still one of the best books on the *Odyssey*, is W. J. Woodhouse's *The Composition of Homer's Odyssey* (Oxford, 1930), which focuses on folklore elements. D. L. Page's *The Homeric Odyssey* (Oxford, 1955) and *Folktales in Homer's Odyssey* (Cambridge, MA, 1973) reveal wonderful material, although as an Analyst Page never quite gets the point.

Other books of general interest include A. Thornton, *People and Themes in the Odyssey* (London, 1970), with many insights, and S. Murnaghan, *Disguise and Recognition in the Odyssey* (Princeton, NJ, 1987), a useful study of this central narrative device. J. S. Clay's *The Wrath of Athena: Gods and Men in the Odyssey* (Princeton, NJ, 1983) is strong on the relationships between divine and mortal in the *Odyssey*. C. Dougherty in *The Raft of Odysseus: The Ethnographic Imagination of Homer's Odyssey* (Oxford, 2001) ties the *Odyssey* to the rapidly changing social and economic life of the eighth century BC. S. Schein's *Reading the Odyssey: Selected Interpretive Essays* (Princeton, NJ, 1995) has essays by important critics, some translated into English for the first time.

The theme of sexual conflict has inspired worthwhile studies of sexual roles and relationships, for example B. Cohen, ed., *The Distaff Side: Representing the Female in Homer's Odyssey* (Oxford, 1995). Nancy Felson-Rubin, *Regarding Penelope: From Character to Poetics* (Princeton, NJ, 1994), combines audience-oriented criticism with psychological analysis to study Penelope's character.

The *Odyssey* has defined the West's self-image as the questing explorer of the unknown and inspired countless literary recreations. W. B. Stanford's *The Ulysses Theme: A Study in the Adaptability of a Traditional Hero* (Oxford, 1963) is a good account. For a more modern treatment there is H. Bloom's much shorter *Odysseus/Ulysses* (New York, 1992).

Index